SPIRITUAL AMNESIA:

A Wake Up Call to What You Really Are

LAUREN SKYE

Sketches by Emma Ocean

PRAISE FOR LAUREN SKYE

This book is a practical user's guide to the spiritual self. Lauren is a master teacher of spiritual tools that awaken you to the aspects of your life and reality that you know are true but have struggled to harness. Readers will find clarity and aliveness as they come out from being "deep in the fog of forgetfulness" and rediscover their true nature."
—Brian Gast, Executive Coach and author of *The Business of Wanting More: Why Some Executives Move from Success to Fulfillment and Others Don't*

"Very few spiritually based authors write at the high level of Lauren Skye. *Spiritual Amnesia: A Wake-Up Call to What You Really Are* is the kind of instruction manual that should be required reading by any seeker of truth. Her chapters are rich and each one is like a thread that weaves through her fabric of work, to make its indelible mark on our minds. This book doesn't seek to show what Lauren Skye already knows, it seeks to take us on a journey with her.

She has a clear style and uses it to make the ineffable accessible. She's not just writing down affirmations that we hear every day, she invites us to enter the world of real energy and allow her to guide us to tangible changes on the level of miracles.

A masterpiece of applicable techniques geared to expand us beyond where we are used to being, written by a woman that we can trust, I know this from direct experience because I sat in her classroom.

Thank you Lauren Skye, your timing is perfect."

—Mark S. Husson, Author, *LoveScopes, What Astrology Already Knows About You and Your Loved Ones,* and founder of 12Radio.com

"Fortunately, we have in our world courageous souls dedicated to helping us open our mind-gates to a more expanded awareness and to the joyous celebration that is our life. Lauren Skye is one of them, and she does this through her ability to give our deeper being permission to step forth and let its true light shine. She speaks to our spiritual growth with clarity, certainty, honesty and warmth."

—Michael J Tamura, Spiritual Teacher, Clairvoyant Visionary and Author of *You Are the Answer: Discovering and Fulfilling Your Soul's Purpose*

"Lauren Skye's deeply personal stories and journey are excellent examples of how we can learn and evolve. *Spiritual Amnesia* is full of wonderful tools to learn about ourselves, from eye-opening insights to meditation techniques for just about every life situation. Lauren teaches us how, by working with our energy, we can clear out wounds and blocks to help us open more fully to the intertwined nature of our physicality and spirituality."

—Terry Chriswell, publisher, *Mile High Natural Awakenings*, and author, *Moving Toward Happy*

TABLE OF CONTENTS

HAVE YOU FORGOTTEN?

Imagine feeling content. Imagine being free of the chronic undercurrent of tension and stress that seems to plague us all. Imagine knowing without doubt that you belong; in the moment, in your own skin, in the world, in the Universe.

What if the snarled traffic, spilled coffee, and the angry supervisor didn't ruin your day? What if the hassles of child care, family dynamics and the endless to-do lists didn't make your heart race? What if you could breathe, sleep, and even raise a smile as you faced a career shift, a relationship ending, health challenges or money dilemmas? What would your day be like with a sense of true peace, knowing that all is well, no matter what?

This contentment is not only accessible, it's already within you. It's a natural part of who you are. Finding it requires only that you wake up and remember.

Remember that you are indeed a soul on a journey, connected always to the divine. Remember that all that is manifesting around you, both physically and experientially, is a result of your dancing with the immense possibilities of consciousness. Remember that you create reality from the inside out, and that reality is yours to create.

Spiritual Amnesia: A Wake-Up Call offers a path to a joyous, abundant life. Through inspirational teachings, the sharing of transformative personal experiences, and practical, how-to techniques, Lauren Skye reframes the experience of life from pain to joy, from challenge to adventure.

The soul-calling practices she offers in the form of easy, accessible meditations and "imaginings" transform the insights she shares into lasting change in your everyday world. The exercises are perfect for those new to the concepts of meditation or for those with busy minds and lives. For those already familiar with energy work, the techniques will expand your practice in a wonderful way.

Get ready to look at yourself, your life, and life itself in a whole new way. This book will wake you up from forgetting and guide you gently toward a new perspective. You'll never look back.

Spiritual Amnesia: A Wake-Up Call is a roadmap to a new way of being.

REMEMBERING CHERYL

My friend Cheryl died at the young age of forty-six after a bone marrow transplant we'd hoped would save her. In the final hours, I sat with her in a Denver hospice in the dual role of friend and Minister. During a break from the vigil, I gathered with some of the family in the cafeteria. After half a cup of coffee, I knew it was time to get back to Cheryl's room, and we all hurried to return as a group.

Cheryl's unconscious body emitted a jarring, weighted, snore-like sound with each gasp of breath. She had been breathing this way for hours. I sat beside her, held her hands, looked at her beautiful face and then gave up my chair. The man who had been her long-term partner came, sat and held.

I moved to where I could see both Cheryl's physical body and her energetic body, in one of the upper corners near the ceiling. Family and friends filed in. I looked back and forth from bed to ceiling, acknowledging the body and the being of light that had created it. Things grew strangely calm in the room, and the conversation drifted to stories from Cheryl's sisters about farting contests they had as children. Everyone erupted into laughter and I turned to Cheryl at the ceiling. "See, Cheryl," I said aloud, "you've healed your family."

At that moment her harsh, labored breathing stopped, Cheryl smiled from the ceiling, and the eruption of laughter transformed into an explosion of pain as those gathered began the journey of letting go.

I see Cheryl still. Our friendship continues in a different way. There are stretches when she visits frequently in my meditations, always radiating contentment and offering words of encouragement. Sometimes, I don't see her for months at a time. I know she'll be there when it's my time to watch from the ceiling.

Why are we here? To be ourselves fully, to express our unique gifts, talents and the wisdom we carry. It is our contribution to the whole.

Equally important, we are here to love each other into doing the same.

Most spiritual orders speak of a version of heaven, or nirvana. A place where there is peace, unconditional love, light and no pain. Perhaps nirvana is a place. Perhaps, even more, it's a condition. The condition of knowing oneself in totality, as a soul, as a being of light, a part of the all-one consciousness and at the same time, unique.

Perhaps our over-arching mission is to love into being the creation of heaven on Earth.

How? By bringing spiritual awareness through to our incarnated state; by bringing the beauty and contentment of full awareness into physical form through thought, emotion, words and action. Imagine a planet vibrating at the light and love of spirit.

We start from within ourselves. We clear the way for our own internal heaven, and cultivate the willingness to hold the light for others.

Cheryl transformed her life with spiritual awareness during our years together. She shifted a childhood of pain into a life of joy and contentment. Even as she faced death, she walked with immeasurable grace and peace.

What will knowing yourself as spirit do for you? How will your life change as you experience the truth of what you are? Let's find out together.

INTRODUCTION

Spiritual amnesia is an epidemic. Many of us are in chronic pain, questioning what it all means whether we're driving to work or sitting at the Thanksgiving table. Major life change brings catastrophe when something we treasure is taken away—a job, marriage, even the life of a loved one. Spiritual amnesia creates the emptiness you feel at night, home alone, or sometimes even when you're surrounded by people.

We have forgotten we are spiritual beings on a human journey. Forgetfulness is a catchy disease. We are bombarded with amnesia by a culture that doesn't acknowledge levels of reality beyond the five senses. We catch it by being taught that success and fulfillment come from particular material possessions or social statuses. We get it through traditional religions and their controlling games of punishment and reward.

You are a spiritual being on a human journey. You exist across a span of reality.

In our physical world we can see, hear, touch, taste and smell. In another layer there exists the world of atoms and particles; vibrating, living forms that set the foundation for the physical. Yet another layer is the realm of energy, of information, of non-material yet very real forces that lay the template for the particulate layer and the physical experience.

All of reality exists across a span of forms, and so do you. You are both a Human Self and a Spirit Self. On one level of reality, here you are, a personality and a physical body, reading a book. Your life involves interacting with the physical world and other personalities around you. But that's not all there is to you. You also exist as energy, as does everyone and everything else.

Spiritual amnesia involves forgetting about the realm of energy, the realm from which you've created your Human Self. When you have it, it seems like life is just happening day to day with occasional moments of happiness and love. You try to do things "right;" you eat well, work hard, be a good parent, friend, partner. But there's a missing exuberance, vitality and natural contentment.

What's absent is knowing yourself as energy, the Spirit Self. The experience of knowing self as spirit brings a fulfillment that's hard to describe and can't be replaced. Without knowing what's missing, we try to plug the hole that only self-awareness can fill with money, relationships, status and a myriad of other substitutions. It never works. Still, there's the pain, the sense of being lost. The part that is seeking is seeking itself, the lost awareness of the energetic self.

Being awake means being aware of the realm of energy and of ourselves as energetic beings. When we are awake, life looks, feels and is totally different. Our day may look the same to an outside observer, but we experience contentment, peace, and enjoyment in being alive, no matter what comes our way. **As we become aware of the**

Spirit Self, our sense of ourselves grows larger and larger. Challenges become smaller relative to our range of awareness.

Think of energy as the fabric of reality, with an infinite number of possibilities, like different textures or flavors. Some of the flavors are love, joy, anxiety, worry, peace and contentment, to name just a few. We ourselves are energy as well as physical matter, and the vibrations in our energetic bodies become the seeds of belief. What we believe is true becomes true in our experience. What we believe is the seed of what we think. What we think is the seed of what we feel. Believing is seeing; it's not the other way around.

When we are awake and aware, we see that life happens *through* us, not to us. Our inner landscape of belief, thought and emotion is a result of the energies we carry and is reflected back to us with absolute brilliance in the experiences of life. The energies we carry can be changed, transformed and released when appropriate. And when energy shifts, there's a corresponding shift in our experiences.

When we know ourselves as spiritual beings, we can change the energy we're carrying, evaluate beliefs, question and reframe thoughts, and allow new and different emotional possibilities.

Spirit is a funny word. When I say spirit, I mean the realm in which all of existence is energetic form. I don't mean it in a religious way. All religions at their origin honor the concept of spirit, but there's been so much corruption in the name of control. Putting rules, regulations and hierarchies between the individual and their experience of themselves as energy is a cruel and heartless game.

Discarding religious dogma is clearly a step in the right direction. Threats of eternal damnation for particular behaviors are ridiculous and outdated given our current understanding of the nature of reality and the Universe. Many of us have wisely let go of the dogma. But, we've thrown out the foundation of joy and living well along with the threats of punishment.

Knowingness of the Spirit Self has to be experienced to be recognized. It doesn't always fit into the realm that the thinking mind can embrace and understand. That's why miracles seem impossible. Miracles are movements of energy that exist outside the realm the thinking mind can grasp. We can read about, think about, and talk about energy all day; but until we experience it, we won't know it.

Through this book, I invite you to experience yourself as energy and to bring forth the empowerment and peace that comes from that awareness. I seek to share this with you because I know it will make a tremendous difference in your life and your experience of yourself. **You'll be happier, healthier and more powerful as you tap into yourself as energy**, get to know your Spirit Self and how to interact with the world of energy. As you become aware of all of you, you radiate energy outward that invites others to do the same, spreading a new vibration, replacing amnesia with remembering.

I've structured the material to put the experience of energetic awareness first. In Part One, I'll show how to become aware of energy, how to change energy and how to experience yourself as a spiritual being. In Part Two, we'll talk about how to see things from a spiritual perspective and apply this emerging awareness in your daily life. In Part Three, we'll go even deeper to explore living with conscious spiritual awareness every day.

Welcome to your journey of self discovery and a whole new world. I'm honored to walk beside you.

PART 1 – EXPERIENCING SPIRITUAL AWARENESS

EXPERIENCING SPIRITUAL AWARENESS

CHAPTER 1: BASIC CONCEPTS AND GROUNDING

In this section, I'll describe the foundation skills for experiencing yourself as energy. As you practice them, you'll naturally open up to your Spirit Self.

You may also notice positive changes beginning to happen in your daily life. You'll be calmer, feel more powerful, happier and more resilient when responding to challenges. As you open to the beauty and grace of spirit within you, that unfolding is miraculously mirrored in a renewed sense of strength and joy in the everyday.

Meditation Is a Journey

Let's develop your energetic skills through a series of imaginary journeys, or meditations. If you've tried meditating before but haven't been successful, don't worry. These techniques are simple, fast, easy, and don't require you to stop thinking.

Instead, the meditations redirect your thinking mind toward the world of energy through a series of experiences. Gradually the intellect will let go and gently surrender to a deeper awareness of the miracle within you: your Spirit Self. If your thoughts argue a little bit along the way, don't be surprised.

There's a part of all of us called the "Analyzer." The analyzer likes to figure things out, pick them apart and be certain that everything makes sense. The problem with the analyzer is that it is limited – it's already decided what's true, what can make sense and what fits into a small box of possible realities. If you get any arguments, it will be from this part of yourself.

The techniques we'll be exploring will speak to the larger part of you, beyond the thinker. We'll build a bridge of awareness between the Human Self and Spirit Self. If the analyzer finds this work silly or unreasonable, that's ok. Simply notice those thoughts, try the presented exercise anyway, and notice your inner experience shift.

Life Is a Mirror

Think of the skills you'll learn as energetic "tools," built on the core principal that we are spiritual beings having a human experience. We'll be using the tools to build our bridge of awareness.

We're made of energy, and the flavors of energies we embody influence our lives. We create our lives from the inside out. The vibrations we carry bubble up through the layers of reality to form our beliefs, thoughts and emotions.

Our experience of life is a direct reflection of our beliefs. Remember, believing is seeing, and it all starts with energy. With some simple tools, we access the Spirit Self where the energies we carry can be changed, transformed and released when appropriate. That shift will change our experiences.

To change our experience, we need only change the energy we're carrying, evaluate the beliefs, question and reframe the thoughts, and allow new and different emotional possibilities. We'll use the tools to create the shift. It really works!

Here are a couple of tips for getting the most out of the experience. First, please don't push or rush yourself or the process. Give yourself room to practice the techniques and let awareness emerge. It's best to go at a relaxed pace, not working too hard, and without hurrying to get to the finish line.

Accumulate the Tools You Need

The skills are cumulative. In each chapter of Part 1, we'll build upon the previous skill set, expanding our practice and our awareness. We're building a toolbox of energetic skills that work together. So, it's a good idea to read the chapters and do the exercises in sequential order.

That being said, if you need a break from the learning journey of Part 1, rest by exploring the topics in Part 2. You'll be re-inspired to come back and learn more about the power within you; the power to command your own energy.

I call the process Meditation for Living, because it's so effective in creating our experience of life to the fullest; with joy, abundance and that natural contentment we all seek. **Meditation for Living wakes us up to the reality that we are energetic beings, free to create change and built to experience joy.**

The Meditation for Living program I'll be teaching you here is also available as an audio series, and you can find it on my website; www.laurenskye.com. You can listen to the first track of the program by visiting the site.

As you read through, if you find more audio would be helpful, contact me at lauren@laurenskye.com and I'll send you the full first lesson for free! If you visit laurenskye.com and sign up for the newsletter, you will receive that first lesson automatically.

Imagine Your Way to Remembering

Throughout the process, you'll notice the words: visualize, pretend and imagine. These are interchangeable words that refer to ways you might engage with energy. If you aren't a visual person, that's ok. Just pretend.

As you practice meditation, you might begin to feel drowsy at times. You might even yawn during some of these practices. That's absolutely fine. And, there's no need for your body to be perfectly still. If you fidget, cough or anything during the process, that's all ok.

And last, I invite you to approach the tools with a childlike spirit of adventure. Be curious, and let yourself have fun as you learn. In lightness and laughter, energy flows, so let's just play.

For best results, I'd suggest you read through an exercise or portion of it, then close your eyes and do the meditation. If you'd like, read through it again, and try it again. Practice each tool as much as you'd like. You can't over-meditate!

Let's Get Started

Find a comfortable chair and have a seat. Place your feet flat on the floor and close your eyes. Take a breath, and another, deeper breath. One more. Notice if you are compelled to get up and do something. If so, please simply notice that without acting on the idea. It's just energy. If you stay in the chair, it will pass.

Notice that just closing your eyes for a few moments is a meditation in itself. By simply closing our eyes, we disconnect from the constant stream of visual input coming into our brains. There's more space to become aware of the inner world.

With your eyes closed, simply begin to notice your body; take a quick inventory of the sensations you feel and the thoughts in your head, without having to change them.

The body is always communicating about the energies you're carrying. The communications come in the forms of physical sensation, thoughts and emotions. Just notice, breathe and listen to what's going on within you. Sit with yourself for just a few moments. This doesn't have to take long, but it's very powerful.

The Imaginary Grounding Cord

Now, let's ground. The foundation skill of the Meditation for Living process is called grounding. It's the first tool we'll be placing in your energetic toolbox. Grounding is simply an imaginary connection from the base of your spine to the center of the Earth (see Illustration 1). Here's how to do it:

With your eyes closed, become more aware of your back, spine and the base of your spine. Imagine a colored beam of light of any color but white or black, extending from the base of your spine, just like a tail would. (I'll address white and black in just a moment.)

The colored beam of light grows from the spot where, if you had a tail, a tail would grow. This spot is the back of the first chakra energy center. Imagine a tail of light.

Imagine your tail of light growing straight down, through your chair, the floor, the building you're in, into the Earth and all the way to the Earth's center. Imagine it reaching, and connecting with the center of the Earth. Breathe, and notice the sensation of being grounded.

This colored beam of light is called a grounding cord, and it has several purposes. One is to help us be present in the moment, the only time that's real. Another is that the grounding cord becomes a trash chute, a way to release energy you don't need to be carrying instead of recycling that energy over and over and over again. You can even imagine anything you don't need, stress, worrisome thoughts, anxiety, fear, all of it can fall down the beam of light into mother Earth, where it is received, recycled and transmuted into neutral creative resource energy. Take a breath... let the grounding cord work for you, you don't have to monitor or check on it.

Colors other than white or black are best for grounding. White tends to rev us way up, and black often moves us toward sleepiness. If you are compelled to use white, try tinting it just a tiny bit to perhaps a light-light blue or light-

light yellow, or very light lavender. If you are drawn to use black, try brown, or a deep blue or slate grey, and see how your body responds.

Grounding Review

Grounding is the creation of an energetic connection from the first chakra energy center of the body to the center of the Earth. The image of the connection is called a grounding cord.

Notice when you ground, your body feels different. Your emotions and thoughts might begin to change. All you did was imagine. When you visualize energetic forms, such as the grounding cord, you are creating energetically. What you imagine becomes real.

Now, let's evolve the grounding tool.

Customize Your Cord

In the last exercise, you used a colored beam of light as a grounding cord. But you can use any image you like; any image that works for you as a conduit for energy; like a strong root, a tree trunk, a plant stem, a pipe, even an animal tail... anything at all that you can imagine.

Try it now. Close your eyes, place your feet on the floor and take a big breath.
Notice the difference when all that visual input you've been receiving is put on pause for a time.

Notice your body... your head, face and neck, your shoulders, arms and torso, your hands, your legs, your feet. Noticing your body and the constant stream of communication it provides helps you relax and become present in the moment.

Specifically notice your spine and the base of your spine, that's the location of the back of the first chakra energy center. Generally, chakras are energy centers in the spiritual body, and they house different types of information and abilities. We'll talk a lot more about them in Chapter 4.

The first chakra, at the base of your spine, is also called the root chakra. Notice that root chakra in your body. It's the spot where, if you had a tail, your tail would grow from. Grounding is a matter of visualizing, imagining or pretending that a cord grows from your first chakra to the center of the earth.

Go ahead and visualize a colored beam of light, or tree root, or plant stem, or pipe, or tail or whatever you'd like, extending from your first chakra and growing downward; through your chair, the floor and the building you're in.

Imagine the grounding cord moving deep into the Earth, through the layers of soil and rock, all the way to the center of the Earth. Imagine the cord reaching the center of the Earth and connecting there.

At the Earth's core, there is molten lava. But if you'd like, you could imagine a different picture to represent the center of the Earth for you to ground into. For example, I like to envision a field of flowers at the center of the Earth. I grow my tree trunk grounding cord all the way down and root into the field that represents the center of the Earth.

Any image will work that works for you to make the connection easy and real. In my years of teaching, I've heard many creative ideas; including an ocean at the center of the Earth that the grounding cord anchors into; a pile of rocks that the grounding cord wraps around, a crystal cave that the cord winds into; even an open socket that the cord plugs into. Maybe some of these will inspire you; or maybe you like the field of flowers image.

Grow your grounding cord all the way to the center of the Earth, and make the connection there with whatever image you'd like. If you don't like the way it feels, you can always start over and play with a new image; or simply see your grounding cord merge with the lava core of the Earth as it exists in physical reality.

Notice the sensation of being grounded. Grounding helps us be present, more clear-headed, more calm and less reactive. Grounding also gives the body a way to release energy it doesn't need to be carrying. Take a breath. Allow anything you don't need to be carrying to drop down the grounding cord.

Have you been stressed, worried, or anxious? These energies can be released into the Earth where they are welcomed, recycled and transmuted into neutral creative force.

Great job! This might be a good time to stand and stretch. When you do, your grounding cord may fall away, or it might stay in place. Either way is fine for now.

More Grounding?

Are you ready for more? Find a comfortable spot to sit and close your eyes. Take a couple of deep breaths. Notice if your grounding cord is still connected. Or, maybe it's connected to you, but not attached to the center of the Earth. Use your imagination and guess if the grounding cord is still there. Imagining and guessing open you up, cracking the doorway to spiritual awareness.

Whatever the case, even if the grounding cord is still well connected, would you imagine releasing it, and let it fall to the center of the Earth for recycling. Releasing an old grounding cord and making a new one is great practice, and re-grounding is an effective way to reset and refresh yourself.

Let's do it. Close your eyes and make a brand new grounding cord for yourself. Maybe you want to play with the same image as before, or try something new.

Imagine that beam of colored light, pipe, root or whatever image you'd like; extending from the first chakra energy center at the base of your spine and growing down through your chair, the floor, the building and the layers of the planet all the way to the Earth's center.

See the grounding cord connect to whatever image you like to represent the center of the Earth. Settle into it, and let your body release and relax.

The Release Button

Next, we'll add two pieces to make the grounding cord even more effective.

The first is the idea of a power switch. Imagine, somewhere on your grounding cord, a switch, like a light switch, a button or a lever. So, yes, you may have a blue beam of light for a grounding cord with a light switch on it! Energy doesn't have to always make logical sense, and often doesn't. So let yourself play, and you'll see that it really does work.

The switch will have an "on" setting, and when you turn your switch on, it powers the grounding cord to begin drawing out energy you don't need, helping you cleanse even more. Create the switch with your imagination and turn it on. This is called "putting the grounding cord on release." Feel the gentle pull. Let me be clear that putting your grounding cord on release does NOT mean you are releasing the cord itself, you are instead strengthening the cord's ability to help you release energy you don't need.

Try it. How does it feel? Do you feel more solid in the chair? Notice the invitation to let go, and accept.

Sometimes when we work with energy and the images don't make logical sense, resistance can arise. The analyzer within you may push back from the process. If this happens for you, let it come, and let it go. Why not try it anyway, even if it seems silly? Why not let go, let the Earth support you, and see what happens next. Maybe your body would feel calmer, your mind a little clearer, as you begin to relax into a gentler state of consciousness.

Timestamp Your Grounding Cord

You're doing a great job. There's just one more piece to this grounding process, and it's about strengthening our ability to be in present time. We'll simply add the current date to the grounding cord. Date stamp it, or write the date in elegant letters somewhere on the cord.

Again, this may seem silly, but it really works. You may have a tree trunk grounding cord with a button power switch and fancy gold numbers for the date.

Dating the grounding cord helps us be in the now, the only time that's real in the physical world. It invites us forward from the past and into freedom from decisions we've made about who we are and what's possible based on the past. It brings us back from the future, which hasn't been created yet and can only be created moment-to-moment, from here and now.

Great work! This is the completion of the grounding process.

Let me sum it up (see Illustration 2).

• Imagine a grounding cord extending from your first chakra energy center at the base of your spine.

• Watch the cord grow all the way to the center of the Earth and connect it there using whatever image you like to represent the Earth's core.

• Add the power switch, putting the grounding cord on release, powering the grounding cord to help you let go.

• Add the present time date, inviting yourself right into the moment.

Take a breath, enjoy the sensation of being grounded. Grounding is always Step One of the Meditation for Living process. And, you can also do it just by itself. You can practice grounding anytime, anywhere. You don't have to be sitting with your eyes closed. You could be standing in a line at the store, in a waiting room at an appointment, stopped at a red light driving, or anywhere at all.

Grounding creates the opportunity for change by changing the possibilities of energy flow. Grounding yourself creates broader possibilities within you. Since everything is energy, you can ground anything.

Try this experiment: Before driving, sit in your car for a moment and ground yourself and then ground the car. Create a grounding cord from the bottom of the car to the center of the Earth. Imagine any energy the car has picked up on its many journeys is released, leaving it refreshed and new. Notice how your trip goes with grounding in play.

You can ground anything; cars, houses, computers, any object. If you have a dog, try grounding your dog! They seem to love it. Cats are another story. My cat won't let me ground her, but she will sit right in my grounding cord, under the chair.

The only thing it's not ok to ground is another person. Imagine one of your friends upset and crying. You wouldn't shove a box of tissues right in their face, invading their space. Grounding another person when they haven't asked you to is a boundary violation. Instead, you might sit with your crying friend and softly place the tissue box near their body as an offering.

Inviting others to ground is done in the same way. If you'd like to offer someone a grounding cord, imagine a beam of colored light or any energy construct near their body and going all the way to the center of the Earth. Don't connect it to their spine. Watch what happens. They may physically move right to the spot where you imagined the cord. Or, they may walk away. There's your answer!

Try playing with grounding and bringing this tool into your day. See what happens.

Remember, the first lesson of the Meditation for Living program is available to you for free. You can listen to the first track of that lesson by visiting the website laurenskye.com. Contact me at lauren@laurenskye.com or visit the site and sign up for the newsletter to receive the full first lesson.

EXPERIENCING SPIRITUAL AWARENESS

CHAPTER 2: CENTER OF HEAD AND THE SIXTH CHAKRA

The second step of our Meditation for Living process is opening the 6th chakra energy center. The sixth chakra is part of your Spirit Self. It sits in the middle of your head; behind your eyes and between your ears.

The sixth is sometimes referred to as the third eye. However, the chakra itself is deep inside your head. The third eye on the forehead represents a gateway into the sixth. The pineal gland, which sits in the mid-brain area, is the physical equivalent of this chakra. The sixth houses our clear energetic vision, sometimes called our clairvoyant ability.

We're All Clairvoyant

Clairvoyance can be a highly-charged word, but this natural vision isn't about predicting the future or dabbling in fortune telling. It's simply a natural awareness of energy and of ourselves as energy. With an open sixth chakra, we can step aside from the daily illusion and begin to connect with our Spirit Self.

We can see our own truth, path and answers; all of which may be unique to us. **Sometimes people hope to see the future, but what's upcoming is not only unknown, it's unknowable.** We create moment-to-moment through our free will and freedom to change and to choose. So, until a particular potential collapses into physical reality as we make choices, anything and everything is possible.

With our own sixth chakras open, we begin to build access to the wisdom of the Spirit Self. We can be clearer about our choices and decisions, and more at peace with our histories. We can see what's influencing us, both in positive and negative ways, and be free to step away from what's not helpful.

Ground First

It's easy to open the sixth chakra. Simply close your eyes, ground, and place your attention there. If you aren't currently grounded, pause here, close your eyes, and ground yourself as described in Chapter 1. Here's a quick review of the process:

• Imagine a grounding cord extending from your first chakra energy center at the base of your spine.
• Watch the cord grow all the way to the center of the Earth and connect it there using whatever image you like to represent the Earth's core.
• Add the power switch, putting the grounding cord on release, powering the grounding cord to help you let go.
• Add the present time date, inviting yourself right into the moment.

Grounding is the foundation tool of the Meditation for Living process. Without it, the other tools become challenging and less effective. Once you have a new grounding cord in place, you don't have to monitor it. Simply create it, and then let it work for you.

Open the Center of Head

Next, play with the idea of being in the middle of your head. Our attention can be anywhere, or "anywhen," and is often scattered in many places and across time. By focusing attention in the middle of our heads, we can come to a calm place of wisdom within. Try it. Be in the middle of your head now. As you do, your sixth chakra will naturally open.

Some folks find it challenging to hold focus in a single spot. If you'd like, you could imagine the idea of a room to represent the center of your head; call it a center of head room (see Illustration 3).

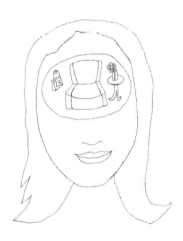

With your imagination, you can decorate this room any way you'd like. My center of head room is pretty simple, it has a chair and table, and the table has a vase of roses on it. There is one window that looks out over a vast ocean and another that looks out over majestic mountains. Since it's my imaginary room, I can have both those views side-by-side.

Only one thing doesn't belong in your center of head room, and that's somebody else. So, no company in there; no friends, family, pets, guides, lovers or others. It's a place just for you. Since your own information is unique to you, we want this space to be housing just your energy. You may see the room around you with your imagination, or you might see yourself sitting in the room. Either way is fine.

Command Central

The center of head room is your command center, where you'll go to work with energy and connect with the wisdom of your Spirit Self. It isn't a heart space, or inner child sanctuary. Those are wonderful spaces, but the center of head space is something different.

It's command central, where you'll practice your ability to see and change energy with intention. It's a place of clarity and calm, where we can come out of the stories we tell ourselves about who we are and how the world works. We can begin to see a broader range of ourselves and our possibilities of experience. In order to change our stories about ourselves, what we tell ourselves about ourselves without even realizing it, we need to get some space from the stories. The center of head is the place to do just that.

Be in the middle of your head. Create your imaginary room. Things may quiet in your inner landscape of thought and feeling. Like grounding, you can go to your center of head space anytime, anyplace. It's a great way to reset your energy and allow new possibilities in any situation.

Meet the Gold Sun

At this point, you've been releasing a lot of energy through your grounding cord. Let's replace that energy you released with energy you'd rather have. Would you become aware now of an energy you'd like to experience more frequently. Maybe you'd like more love, joy, fun, contentment, peace, prosperity or clarity. You'd probably like all of them, but pick one for now, or another word you can think of that represents what you'd like to have more of in your life.

Here is a fun and easy way to bring that energy right into your body and your experience: imagine a big golden ball of light above your head, like a big, golden sun. Imagine writing the word that represents what you want to receive right across the sun.

Watch what happens with your imagination; the golden sun is neutral energy. Writing the word across it is like dropping food coloring into water. The sun will absorb the word and match it, becoming a big golden ball of the vibration you desire.

Now, imagine the sun setting right into your body and the golden light being absorbed by the cells of your body. Let that gold light, now vibrating at the particular flavor of energy you've chosen, come in and fill you; filling your head, neck, and shoulders, your arms, chest and torso, your hands, legs, and knees, all the way down to your feet. If there's more, let it spill around you, surrounding your body (see Illustration 4).

When you're done, take a breath and open your eyes. Notice if you feel different. If you'd like to close your eyes, re-find the center of your head and bring in some more gold suns, go for it! Afterward, you'll go about your day with a renewed sense of both peace and enthusiasm.

EXPERIENCING SPIRITUAL AWARENESS

CHAPTER 3: BOUNDARIES AND CHANGING ENERGY

Now it's time to learn about energetic boundaries and take more steps to intentionally shift the energies we carry and connect with our Spirit Self.

You are creating your meditation practice and building your toolbox. Through this practice, you're building the bridge of awareness between your Human and Spirit Self.

As you do, it's important to be happy with yourself. When you are happy with yourself, the practice is smoother and easier. **When you are in self-judgment, trying to fix yourself, everything gets rough, including meditation.** So, be happy with yourself. It's a choice.

Another piece to consider is the environment in which you meditate. Create an atmosphere for success, with a comfortable place to sit and as few distractions as possible. Close the door, silence your phone or other devices, and take some time just for you. You might want to have water nearby.

Ground First

Grounding is always step one in meditation.

If you aren't grounded right now, let's start there. Even if you are already grounded, consider the idea of dropping the old connection and creating a brand new one. Releasing a grounding cord and creating a fresh one is a great way to reset your energy, refresh yourself and, of course, to practice grounding.

Here's a summary of the steps:

- Imagine a grounding cord extending from your first chakra energy center at the base of your spine.
- Watch the cord grow all the way to the center of the Earth and connect it there using whatever image you like to represent the Earth's core.
- Add the power switch, putting the grounding cord on release, powering the grounding cord to help you let go.
- Add the present time date, inviting yourself right into the moment.

Take a breath, and enjoy the sensation of being grounded.

Something New

Let's add a step here. Notice if the grounding cord needs to be wider than it currently is. Just guess. If so, would you let your body bring the grounding cord to the width that's just right for you right now? Let the body, in its wisdom, decide for you. If you're not sure, you could try widening your cord just a bit, and see how it feels.

Come Into the Center of Your Head

Next, find the middle of your head. Walk into your center of head room. See the room around you, or see yourself in the room, whichever way comes naturally to you. Would you imagine changing one thing about the room to freshen it? Perhaps the color of a wall or placement of a picture or object. Changing something about the center of your head room refreshes your awareness of it, and invites you even more into present time.

Scattered Energy

Great job! Now, let's talk about boundaries. Many of us understand the need for healthy personal, or emotional, boundaries. Good boundaries keep us from being violated. And, they help us not become overly involved in what isn't ours. We can have healthy energetic boundaries too, or a lack thereof.

Without energetic boundaries, it's easy to become scattered and disconnected from the innate wisdom of the Spirit Self. And, it's easy to pick up, carry and become the effect of energies that aren't our own.

Let's say you leave your home in the morning in a good mood; you're looking forward to your day. Then, there's the commute, and folks who drive like they're in a video game; or, perhaps you have a stressful morning meeting, followed by a challenging encounter with clients and a call from a family member in distress. By lunch, you're ready to go home and crawl under the covers.

What happened to your energy? Perhaps it became scattered in all these events.

It's draining to be scattered, because we continue to engage our energy wherever we are. And, carrying other people's energy doesn't help us create our lives according to our own path. It's like putting the wrong gas in your car. The vehicle won't run at its best, and might end up just sputtering along.

Here's a great technique to gather your energy from the scatter, and to create an effective energetic boundary at the same time.

A Rose Is A Rose Is A Rose

Be grounded and sit in the middle of your head. Then, imagine a beautiful rose in front of you. A rose of any color, created by your intention to imagine it. What a beautiful symbol the rose is; the elegant shape, the amazing scent, the seemingly infinite unfolding of the petals. As an energetic symbol and tool, roses have many uses in the Meditation for Living paradigm. One use is to find the furthest away point of our scatter.

The rose itself is an energetic symbol, yet another tool. When we begin to work with the concept of creating energetic symbols, one of the most important things to know is how to let them go. Creating and destroying are two sides of the same coin.

You're looking at this beautiful rose before you. Would you imagine tossing it up into the sky and destroying it? Perhaps you might see the rose explode into a beautiful fireworks display. Let the light of the explosion dissipate and the symbol be no more.

Create and Destroy

Great work! If you find yourself uncomfortable with the concept of destroying, consider this: if we won't destroy, or let go, our lives and our energetic space can become cluttered with out-of-date creations. Letting go makes room for the next step. On the other hand, if we won't create anew, it's hard to let go, because there's that fear; what if there's nothing else? So, the simple meditation of creating and destroying roses helps free up our energetic flow.

You might try it for a few moments right now. Close your eyes and see a beautiful rose before you... notice its shape, its color and the opening of the flower. Now release it, toss it away, high in the sky, and watch it explode into beautiful light. Watch the light fade, and allow that the rose is destroyed.

If you'd like, try it again, maybe with roses of different colors, to become comfortable with the concept of create and destroy. This concept will be important later on as well, as our journey of conscious spiritual awareness continues.

Rose Boundaries

Now, back to the idea of gathering our energy from the scatter and creating our energetic boundary. Close your eyes and create a brand new rose in front of you. This time, instead of destroying the rose, send it off to find the furthest away place you've scattered your energy.

This might be a physical place. Or, it might be someone else's energy field – perhaps someone you love or someone you resist. It might be a point in time, back in the past or off into the future.

You might know where your rose landed, or you might not. It's fine either way. After sending the rose off, call it home, like a rubber band snapping back, only not so fast.

Sending off the rose is like casting a fishing net, then pulling the net in to surround you. You interact with the rose, but your whole energy field around you is affected. As the rose comes home, the energy field around you, sometimes called your aura, is called in, and forms a protective bubble all around you.

Have the rose come back to a point about an arm's length out in front of you. So, the rose will be in front of you and the bubble all around you. Think of a holiday snow-globe, with you inside.

Imagine that the very bottom of the globe connects with your grounding cord as it heads into the Earth. Like a hollow lollipop on a stick, the stick is the grounding cord, the lollipop is the bubble around you, and you are the delicious center. With the bubble grounded too, energy can ground directly out of the bubble itself if needed.

The rose in front represents the edge of your energetic space. It's like a signpost saying "my space begins here." It's both a protective mechanism, deflecting energies that come toward you, and it's a reference point for keeping your own energy grounded and at home in your present time body and aura.

Let's make the rose more effective by grounding it. Would you look at that rose out in front of you and imagine its stem growing longer, longer, longer. Grow the stem all the way to the center of the Earth and connect it. The rose is now a grounded protection rose.

Protection Roses

The grounded protection rose sits at the front of your aura, but the aura bubble is all around you. Our next step is to make copies of the front rose at specific points around the aura bubble to create a protective grid of energy.

With your imagination, make a copy of the rose in front of you and place it about an arm's length behind you, at the back of your aura. You could create the copy in front of you and then move it to the back or you could simply create it behind you. Once the copy is in place at the back of your aura, ground it, by extending its stem all the way to the center of the Earth.

Good work. Next, create a copy of that front rose off to the right or left side of your aura, at about an arm's length distance away from your body, and ground that copy. Now, create a copy of the front rose off to the other side, and ground it.

Let's keep going. Create a copy of this front rose at the top of your aura bubble, about an arm's length above your head. When you extend its stem to the center of the Earth, you could wrap the stem around the outside edge of the bubble, or you could bring it right through the aura bubble. I like to wrap the stem around the outside. Play with it, and notice what you like.

There's one more. The final rose goes at the bottom of your aura bubble, about an arm's length below your feet. It's energy, so it doesn't matter if that point is under the floor. Go ahead and imagine it, and then ground that rose by extending its stem to the center of the Earth.

Right now you are grounded, with a grounding cord connected from the base of your spine to the center of the Earth. Your sixth chakra is open; you're sitting in your center of head room; your aura bubble is all around you and your roses are up, creating a protective energy grid around you (see illustration 5).

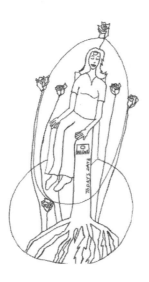

Finding Your Space

This is called being in your space, or finding your space. I encourage you to find your space before you begin your day, or even a few times throughout your day, and notice what happens. You'll feel more energized, happier, and more yourself. And, it will be easier to let things go instead of getting caught up it in conflicts or problems.

Notice what it's like to be in your space. It might be comforting. It might be unfamiliar. If it is unfamiliar, let yourself feel the newness of it all, and acquaint yourself with your own energy and your Spirit Self.

As you may recall, when working with energy, it's an important concept that the energies we carry in our space define our experience of life, and of ourselves. Vibrations carried at the level of the Spirit Self bubble up through the layers of reality to manifest in present-time thoughts, feelings and sensations.

We can change our experience by changing the energies we carry. Now that we've defined our space, we can become proactive about the energies we carry in it.

We've already done that to a degree. We've allowed the grounding cord to draw out energies we don't need to be carrying, and, we've used the gold suns to bring in vibrations we'd like to experience.

Clean Your Spiritual House

Now, let's look at a new way to clean out what we don't need, and replace those vibrations, or frequencies of energy, with energies we'd like to experience.

Take a moment to notice your reality, your inner landscape of thought, emotion, sensation and experience. In that inner reality of yours, what's one energy you'd like to let go of? What's an energy you'd like to release? Maybe you'd like to experience a lot less worry, stress, anxiety or pain.

Imagine a container in front of you, in your energy field, or aura. Here is where you will release this unwanted energy. The container could be a small bubble floating inside your aura bubble, it could be a balloon, perhaps a golden trash bag or any other type of form you can imagine. In a recent class, we had a woman who used shoe boxes as containers to release into, and that worked for her. As you play and practice, you'll find what works for you.

Write the name of the vibration you'd like to release on the container, labeling it. Write 'worry,' or whatever word you're working with across the balloon, bubble, trash bag or whatever type of container you're envisioning.

If you aren't sure what to release, you could simply create a container and label it: "Any energy I don't need right now."

Now, allow the vibration you're releasing to move from your body and energy field into the container.

All you need do is intend and be willing. Even if there are many reasons this vibration exists in your world, imagine letting the vibration itself go. Step aside from the reasons, just for now, and fill the container with the energy you'd like less of in your life.

When the container is full, imagine tossing it high in the sky. Imagine destroying the container by blowing it up, disintegrating it, or however you'd like to extinguish this symbol. The energy is now released and transmuted.

You now have two ways to release energy. You can allow it to flow down your grounding cord, or you can put it in a container and release it.

Notice what vibration you would like to experience instead of the one you just let go of. Maybe you'd like to experience more clarity, joy, fun, prosperity, contentment or peace. Pick a vibration now, any one you'd like. Remember the golden sun from Chapter Two?

Bring In a Gold Sun

Imagine a big golden ball of light above your head, a big gold sun. The sun will be so big that part of it will be inside your aura bubble, and part of it will extend above the bubble. Imagine writing the word that represents what you want to receive right across the sun. Watch what happens; the golden sun is neutral energy. Writing the word across it is like dropping food coloring into water. The sun will absorb the word and match it, becoming a big gold ball of the flavor of energy you desire.

You might be tempted to put a bunch of words in your sun, creating a salad sun, mixing different flavors. However, the suns are most effective with one vibration at a time, so you can really experience, and get to know the particular energy. You can always bring in more suns of different words, one after the other.

Now, imagine the sun setting right into your body and the golden light be absorbed by the cells of your body. Let that gold light, now vibrating at your desire, come in and fill you; filling your head, neck and shoulders; your arms, chest and torso; your hands, legs and knees; all the way down to your feet and toes. If there's more, let it spill into the aura around you, setting your environment at the energy you'd like as well.

Bring In a Sun, Repeat

Repeat this process a few times. Create a golden sun, set it at a particular frequency of energy with a word and then fill in.

Try it again; create the sun, choose your word, put the word in the sun and bring it in through your body and aura.

Pretty soon, you will notice a change in how you feel. That change has come from changing your energy.

Unmerge and Define

Another type of energy that's good to let go of and clean out of your space is energy from other people. It's natural to merge energies with others, both those we love and those we resist. It's a part of life.

As unique souls, it is healthy to sometimes take a break from the merge, and just be ourselves. This is more important for sensitive people who tend to pick up the energies of others more frequently. **Sensitive's need to be able to know the difference between their own energy and someone else's.** That's so important in being able to find and enjoy our own path, truth and joy. We can't do it if we're always carrying someone else in our space. As I mentioned earlier, it's like the wrong gas for your car. Your body is your vehicle in this life. It runs best on your own energy.

We'll clean out other people's energy in much the same way as vibrations we don't need, but with a slight twist. Let's try it right now.

First, be in your space; grounded, in your center of head room, cozy inside your bubble with your roses up.

Notice a person whose energy you carry. This might be someone close, or someone who is a challenge in your world. Imagine a container before you; a bubble, balloon, maybe even imagine a rose as a container, like a rose-shaped sponge to soak up the energy. Using roses to clean energy out is yet another of their many uses in the Meditation for Living information set.

So, imagine that bubble, balloon, rose or other container before you as you sit in your space. Create a small picture of the person next to the container, like a snapshot, and slide that photo right into the container. Alternatively, you could write their name next to the container and slide it in. The container is now set at their energy. Let yourself release the energy you're carrying into the container. **Since the container is now set at their energy, it will also attract their vibration out of you.**

When the container is full of their energy, release it. Toss that container high in the sky, and destroy it by seeing it explode or disintegrate, or however else you'd like to destroy it. The container is destroyed, not the other person's energy. Their vibration is released and available to go back to them in divine timing and manner, whenever they are ready for it. It's not your job to give them their energy back directly, that could even be invasive. Your work is to release it to a neutral space and let spirit take over from there.

Call Back Your Energy

Now, create a golden sun above your head. With your intention, consciously call back your energy from their space into the sun. It's always a two-way street. If someone has energy in your space, you most likely have energy in theirs.

Calling your essence home makes the energy available for you. See the sun above your head; you might even want to put your own name in the sun if that feels right. Be willing to call your energy home. All you need to do is intend and be willing. Watch the sun fill with your unique vibration. When it's nice and full, imagine the sun setting right into your body and the golden light being absorbed by the cells of your body. Let that gold light, you, come in and fill you; filling your head, neck and shoulders; your arms, chest and torso; your hands, fingers, legs and knees; all the way down to your feet and toes. If there's more, let it spill into the aura around you.

You now have two ways to release energy; down the grounding cord, and with containers. And, you have two ways to gather your energy, with the protection rose and with gold suns. You might want to repeat this process, or try it with different people. Enjoy the sensation of experiencing your own unique energy in your own space.

The Toolbox Revisited

We're building a skill set of energy techniques, like a toolbox of energetic tools. So far in your toolbox, you have grounding, the center of head space, the aura bubble, protection roses and the process of create and destroy with containers and suns to affect conscious change.

Each skill has its own purpose, and they come together to create a wonderful, fun and effective meditation process: Meditation for Living. I encourage you to meditate before you start your day, or whenever you can throughout your day.

It doesn't have to take a long time. Ground, find your center of head, set up your bubble and roses, clean yourself out and fill yourself in. With just a little practice, it doesn't take long at all. And, you'll see a big difference in your experience as you become proactive in the management of energy, in your experience of yourself, and of your life.

EXPERIENCING SPIRITUAL AWARENESS

CHAPTER 4: CHAKRAS

Let's take a short break from building the Meditation for Living skill set and talk about chakras. Chakras are energy centers in the spiritual body. The term comes from an ancient Sanskrit word meaning vortex or wheel. These energy centers come into play in our next level of study, so we need to look at them before going further.

Your physical body has organs; the brain, stomach, liver and all the rest. Each organ has a specific purpose. Your Spirit Self has chakras, each with a unique function, and all working together, carrying information that manifests in your reality.

Keeping It Simple

Chakras are complex and beautiful forms of energy. People can spend a lifetime studying them, and some do. Information about the placement and functions of the chakras varies from teaching to teaching.

We can engage with the chakras easily and effectively without years of dedicated learning. A few simple definitions empower us to work with ourselves and create healing and change within the chakra system.

There are seven primary chakras. Think of them as seven circles of energy, each containing a library of information and abilities (see Illustration 6). The chakras are dynamic. They open, close and spin to various degrees.

Each of us is called to find our own truth about chakras. I'll be sharing my truth developed from my own studies and fine-tuned in my experiences of reading and healing others. I invite you to take what fits for you and let the rest go.

Whatever I share, my hope is to inspire you, not convince you. Your life is about finding your truth, the information that's in harmony with you, and so fuels your enthusiasm for living.

Harmony

If we consider the chakras as libraries of information, we could say that some of the information stored in the library is in affinity, or in harmony, with who we are in present time and some of it isn't. Some books we like, some we've read and wouldn't enjoy rereading.

For example, in my journey, I wasn't sure what to do with myself in my young adulthood. No career seemed to call me because I really didn't know who I was. Those were confusing times. I didn't fit in anywhere. So, on my father's advice, I entered the business world, and eventually became a computer programmer.

This worked for a while. At each company, I become the "office therapist." People would stop by my cube to share their troubles. It was satisfying to be helpful. Later, when the social dynamics of the group began to crumble, as social dynamics usually do, I'd leave quietly, taking their secrets with me.

The cycle repeated until I began to find my own unique abilities and information. Then, I was called by my Spirit Self to follow my path more authentically. At that point, I had to let go of my father's truth, face the fear of risk and go for my dreams. Of course, he thought I was crazy for giving up a stable career.

On a chakra level, I had to release my father's energy from my third chakra (the personal power center) in order to manifest my own path. He had loving intentions in his vision for me, and since I had none of my own at that time, it was a good idea to borrow his truth. And, when it was time, it was a good idea to let it go.

First Chakra First

Let's look at each of the chakras and their roles. You'll find a summary of keywords for the chakras later in this chapter.

The first energy center sits at the base of your torso and is sometimes called the root chakra. We ground from the back of this energy center.

The first chakra is well-named. This location carries information about our body's health, vitality and will to live. **Without a healthy first chakra, the body suffers and the human experience is depleted.**

Physical well being, self-preservation, food, water and shelter are examples of first chakra issues. Now, that doesn't mean we won't find energy around these topics in other chakras – it's not that cut and dry. These are simply keywords relating to the type of information the first chakra holds.

The first chakra physically expresses the energies it carries through the body's corporeal sensations. It is closely linked to the sense of smell.

In metaphysical shops and gathering places, you may have seen a rainbow of colors that represent the chakras. The first chakra is represented as red in that spectrum. Some would say a happy first chakra must be red. That hasn't panned out in my experience of spirit. I've seen happy first chakras of all colors, so I discard rules about how an energy center should look.

Second Chakra: Emotions and Sexuality

Your second chakra energy center sits slightly below the belly button level. The vortex itself, as with all the chakras, is deep in the center of the energetic body. The second carries information about our emotions, sexuality, sensuality and empathy.

Many of the joys of being alive are second chakra considerations. Eating a delicious chocolate is a second chakra event.

Empathy, the feeling of other people's emotions is an ability of the second. This is a wonderful capacity, unless you don't know you're doing it and take on those feelings as your own!

The second chakra expresses the energies it carries through the emotions. It is associated with the sense of taste and is represented by the color orange in the chakra color schematic.

Third Chakra: Will and Drive

Your third chakra sits at about diaphragm level, just below the sternum. The third holds data about our personal power, will and drive. I like to call it the action chakra, or do-er.

Ideally, the action of the third chakra brings the vision of the seventh chakra (spiritual truth) at the top of the head into physical manifestation. When someone is disconnected from their seventh, the third chakra often tries to take over. Folks often try to do more in order to be more. Of course, this doesn't work. The contentment of being is naturally accessed through the seventh chakra.

Energies in the third also influence prosperity. The third energy center expresses the energies it carries through both thought and action. In the charka rainbow, this one is yellow.

Fourth Chakra: The Heart

Your fourth chakra sits at the heart level and is sometimes called the heart chakra. At its core, the fourth carries the information about how we see ourselves. That vision of self forms the foundation for all other relationships and our freedom to give and receive love.

The fourth chakra also carries information about relationship issues, affinity with others and past-life connections. But again, and most importantly, **the fourth chakra carries the image of how we see ourselves.**

Take a moment to consider the concept that how you see yourself lays the groundwork for all your relationships and for your whole experience of life. If you see yourself as broken or 'not enough,' that's going to play out everywhere in your experience. **By noticing and changing how you see yourself, you can change your life.** You'll be doing just that as you wake up to who you are as Spirit Self using the Meditation for Living processes as we go forward.

The fourth is also a bridge between the "lower chakras" (first, second and third) and the "upper chakras" (fifth, sixth and seventh). The lower chakras aren't less important than the upper ones. The delineation only marks a difference in the types of information stored. The lower chakras tend to relate more to our human needs and experience, and the upper centers relate more to our spiritual considerations. A happy fourth chakra, carrying a joyful picture of how we see ourselves, brings these two levels together.

The fourth center is linked to our sense of touch. In the rainbow, the heart chakra is green.

Fifth Chakra: Expression

The fifth chakra sits at the base of the throat. This center carries information about communication, both incoming and outgoing. It involves both the inner voice and outward expression. The fifth influences how we communicate with ourselves and with others, and our freedom to do so.

This energy center can be blocked if there has been a lack of safety on a physical, emotional, mental or spiritual level. A foundation of wellbeing supports free-flowing expression.

Additionally, if there is wounding in the other chakras, the function of the fifth will be influenced by that pain. Expression may be "stuck in the throat," so to speak. Or, communications may be tinged with a judgmental or angry tone. The inner voice would be affected as well.

In the natural state of spiritual wellness, the chakras carry information that is in harmony with the present time truth of the Human Self and Spirit Self. The fifth will beautifully reflect that attunement with clean, clear expression.

The fifth chakra is linked to our sense of hearing. It is blue in the chakra rainbow.

Sixth Chakra: Clairvoyance

The sixth chakra sits in the middle of our heads. We've talked about the sixth chakra before. It's the space represented by the center of head room in our meditations. The physical equivalent is the pineal gland in the brain.

The sixth houses our clairvoyant ability, or clear vision. The sixth chakra simply sees what is, without judgment or opinion. It's neutral. With an open, clear sixth chakra, we can see our own truth, path and answers.

This center is linked to our sense of clairvoyance. Everyone has a sixth chakra, so everyone has clairvoyance. Not all souls have an intention to use this ability, but it is within everyone. The color for the sixth is indigo, a deep purple-blue.

Seventh Chakra: Spiritual Truth

The seventh chakra sits at the top of the head. The seventh is also called the crown chakra. It's unique in position. I see the seventh chakra as laying flat on the top of the head. Not all teachers agree, so follow your own truth.

I envision the seventh like a small halo lying on the top of the head. The other chakras are oriented perpendicular to that position. So, if I were looking at you from the front, standing in front of you, I would see the first six chakras as circles and I would see the side edge of the seventh.

This energy center is the first in a series of ring-like structures that sit above your head, creating a pathway in and out of the body and forming the tunnel to the white light we hear about in near-death experiences.

The crown chakra holds information about our unique spiritual truth, our part of the whole. And, the multifaceted crown chakra also holds a catalog of the lower six chakras. If I were to touch a point on the crown, I'd get a response in one of the other six chakras as well.

It is linked to knowingness. The phrase "off the top of my head" is a good example of this chakra in action; it just knows. The seventh is shown as violet or white in the chakra color palette.

The Chakras in Action

The chakras are connected. As energy moves through the Spirit Self, the chakras all contribute to our experience of reality.

Here are two real-life cases of the chakras displaying information that isn't in affinity with the person in present time:

A first chakra example: A client of mine, let's call her Lisa, was in a minor car accident. Just a bumper-to-bumper jolt, nothing too serious. For weeks afterward, Lisa was scared to drive. She white-knuckled it through the relatively harmless streets of Denver. Her first chakra was responding with anxiety, saying, "I'm in danger on a physical level here." We healed it by clearing the first chakra of that energy and replacing it with present time safety.

A third chakra example: A student in our program, "Martha," is a successful business consultant. She has money, status and a great house. Yet, she had been unhappy for years. She has tried to do more, to be more, and to accumulate more to feel safe. It hasn't worked.

Through her spiritual development, Martha is getting in touch with her Spirit Self, becoming less attached to her material stuff and noticing those possessions have nothing to do with her true value as a human being. It's wonderful to watch her become more and more relaxed each week as she meditates and explores her spiritual truth.

Martha is gradually letting the spiritual truth of the crown chakra become the driving force, instead of the material productivity of the third. She'll still have her money and status, along with irreplaceable inner peace. If she keeps up her great work, Martha will truly have it all.

Chakra Keywords and Phrases

The chart below outlines the qualities of each energy center:

1st Chakra: Body, survival, self-preservation
Health, food, water, shelter
Expresses physically
Smell
Red

2nd Chakra: Empathy, sexuality, sensuality
Feeling other people's feelings
Expresses emotionally
Taste
Orange

3rd Chakra: Action, free will, personal power, choice, money, mobility
Manifests vision of the seventh chakra
Expresses mentally and through doing
Sight
Yellow

4th Chakra: How I see myself
Basis of all relationships
Love and affinity of ourselves and others
Bridge between upper and lower
Touch
Green

5th Chakra: Communication
Expression
Inner voice and outward voice
Hearing
Blue

6th Chakra: Neutrality
Seeing what is without judgment
Seeing our path and place in the world
Clairvoyance
Indigo

7th Chakra: Spiritual gateway
Spiritual truth
Perpendicular to other chakras; one of the rings
Catalog of 1st through 6th
Knowingness
Violet or White

A Chakra Meditation

We can begin to engage consciously with the chakras by applying these simple definitions. Combining this information with the spiritual experience of meditation, we create self-awareness, change and healing.

Here's a chakra meditation you can do right now:

Grounding is always step one in meditation. Let's start there. Remember the steps to grounding? Here they are:
- Notice your body and the base of your spine.
- Grow your grounding cord from the base of your spine to the center of the Earth.
- See the cord connect with whatever image you like to use for the center of the Earth.
- Let your body widen the cord to whatever width is right for you right now.
- Create the release switch and set it to the release setting. Let the grounding cord begin to draw out of you any energy you don't need to be carrying.
- Date the grounding cord with the current date.

Next, be in the Center of Your Head:
- Walk in to your center of head room. See the room around you, or see yourself in the room, whichever way works for you.
- Imagine changing one thing about the room to freshen it.
- Check for others' energies and move them out if needed.

Establish your Aura Bubble and Protection Roses:
- Notice if there are old protection roses around you.

- Gather them up, cut their stems, toss them away and destroy!
- Create a brand new rose in front of you.
- Send the new rose off to find the furthest away place you've left energy.
- Call it home.
- Allow the bubble to form around you as the rose comes home.
- Create the five other protection roses and the five additional delineation points around the aura: behind you, to the right, to the left, at the top of your bubble and at the bottom.

As you sit in meditation, become aware of a chakra you'd like to clear. If you have health challenges, work with the first chakra. If you have trouble at work, pick the third. Refer to the summary list above if you need a reminder.

Imagine seeing the chakra as a circle inside your body, similar to an old-style camera shutter, the circular kind that opens and closes. The chakras themselves do open and close.

In our classes, we often use a vegetable steamer for demonstrating the chakras, the metal kind that folds open. It's a good image and kind of fun too. Remember that the vibration of play is always helpful. If you find yourself getting too serious, picture seven tiny vegetable steamers in your body, all spinning and opening and closing like the chakras do. Now try not to smile.

Time to Clean Out

Let's clean out the chakra you've chosen. Imagine an empty energetic container out in front of your body, at the location of the chakra you've chosen. The container could be a small bubble floating inside your aura bubble, or it could be a balloon, or perhaps a golden trash bag. It could be a rose, or any other type of form you can imagine.

With your intention, allow any energy that doesn't serve your highest good for your life to move from the chakra into the container. Just pretend or imagine it happening. What would that look and feel like? You as Spirit Self know how to release. Your mind, your Human Self, can sit back and relax, watch the process with your imagination, or just trust that it is happening.

When the container is full, let it go. Release the balloon, watch the bubble float away, toss the trash bag or rose; and watch it go high into the sky. Now, burst or destroy the container, allowing the energy to be freed and transmuted.

You might want to repeat the cleansing process a few times to let more and more energy go.

Time to Fill In

After you've cleaned out, let's fill in. Imagine a big gold sun above your head. Use a word to fill the sun with whatever energy you'd like to have in that particular chakra. If you're at a loss to choose, how about enthusiasm? Enthusiasm says YES to life with exuberance. That vibration would be a good one for any chakra.

Whatever word you've picked, watch the sun absorb, match and become the energy of the word you've chosen. Let the sun get really big. You could set that sun into your

body as we've done before. Or, try this; imagine popping
the bottom of the sun like poking a water balloon. See the
energy stream from the sun into your body and direct it
right into the chakra you just cleansed, or the general area
of your body where that chakra sits. Let the chakra fill with
your own energy vibrating at the frequency you've chosen,
then let it fill up the rest of you.

A lovely meditation to give to yourself is to clean each
chakra, first through seventh. This takes a little time, but it
is well-spent. If your day allows, you might consider
staying right here and clearing yourself now.

EXPERIENCING SPIRITUAL AWARENESS

CHAPTER 5: FLOWING ENERGY

Now we're going to take it up a notch – a big notch! Our next step is called Flowing Energy, or Running Energy. As we consciously allow and invite energy to flow through us, we bridge our awareness to Spirit Self. We wake up, our eyes clear and the blurriness of amnesia fades more and more.

Running energy is important. It makes everything look and feel different. In my practice, when a student calls in crisis or feeling lost, I always ask, "Have you run your energy?" Or I request, "Please run your energy for fifteen minutes and let's talk after that."

Generally, when energy is flowing, there's more ease, and more opportunity for change, growth and healing. Think of a flowing river. If something gets stuck, like logs or debris, the power of the flow will flush it through. When the river isn't flowing strong enough to clear the clutter, it gets blocked. There's stagnation, build up and things begin to fester. So it is with us.

Running Energy relaxes the body, calms the nervous system and deep cleans the chakras. It also assists us in being in the present moment and supports us in moving in the direction of our dreams. And, it just feels good.

The process can be a bit confusing at first, so we'll take it step-by-step and then put the steps together in the end.

Let's dive right in and do some meditations. Afterwards, I'll talk about how and why it works so well.

A Simple Flow

Take a moment to find your space. Here's a quick review of the steps:
- Ground
  - Create the cord
  - Connect to the center of the Earth
  - Add the release switch and date
- Be in the center of your head room
  - Find your room
  - Change something about it to bring the room to present time
  - Take a moment to clean out others' energies
- Create Your Bubble and Roses
  - Clean out old protection roses
  - Create a new rose to find your energy and call it home
  - Make your copies and ground them

Once you're in a light meditation with the above tools in place, begin to imagine energy from the core of the Earth coming up into your feet and filling your legs. Watch it flow through your body and out the top of your head. Just play with the idea and pretend it's happening.

Now, picture energy from the Universe coming down, into the top of your head, flowing through you and down into the Earth. Let the two currents happen at the same time.

This simple flow meditation can create a sense of peace and belonging.

Experience this for a few moments and then let the flow dissipate, or lessen, in both directions, becoming less and less, until it stops.

Open your eyes. Notice how you feel. Different? Lighter?

A little off-balance? If so, that's ok, it's just a symptom of energy changing. You're starting to hold yourself differently, like putting down a heavy weight that's been carried a long time.

Next, let's refine the process by working this concept of flow within a system of energy channels in the Spiritual Self.

Please know that this process can be challenging at first, and a little confusing.
Expect a little uncertainty and stay with it anyway. I promise the payoff will be beyond worthwhile.

Remember the audio series is available to you as well. You can find and listen to the first track of the program on my website, www.laurenskye.com. And, remember, I'll send you the full first lesson for free. Contact me at lauren@laurenskye.com to receive it, or sign up for my newsletter and links to download the audios will come right to you.

The Earth Energy Flow

For a moment, be aware of your feet. Imagine an opening in the arch of each foot. It's called a foot chakra. You could picture it as an old-style camera shutter, a vegetable steamer or a simple circle.

Let's flex these chakras and wake them up. Imagine opening them. Picture the feet chakras opening all the way up to 90% open. After a moment or two, pretend to close them down to about 10% open. Open and close them a couple of times.

Then, settle them at about 70 or 80% open. Just picture it, or pretend. If you're not sure, simply let go and allow your body and Spirit Self to decide. Trust that your feet chakras will come to the perfect level of openness for you right now.

The camera lens image or vegetable steamer picture work well for engaging with the feet chakras. In reality, the chakra is an opening at one end of a channel and one channel runs through each leg. The channels begin at your feet, run up each leg and end at the first chakra. Think of the channels like hoses or pipes inside your body.

The leg channels are called just that, "leg channels." They are also called Earth channels because they receive and flow energy from the Earth through the body.

Running Earth Energy

While sitting in the center of your head, become aware of the center of the Earth, imagine several colors available there, like different flavors of energy. Ask yourself in your imagination, or ask your body: what's the perfect Earth energy color for me right now? Guess any color, except white or black. Let's leave those alone for now.

All you need do is say yes, and allow it to happen. Watch with your imagination as the color flows up to you. Notice your feet chakras are also drawing it up. See the energy flow through the layers of the Earth, up through the floor of the building you're in and right into your open feet chakras.

Let this Earth Energy fill and flow through your leg channels. It will come up into your feet, up through your ankles, up through your legs to your knees, where it will take a 90 degree turn if you're sitting, then flow through your thighs, into your first chakra and down your grounding cord back to the center of the Earth creating an energetic loop.

Earth energy flows up from the center of the Earth, into your open feet, through the leg channels and down the grounding cord (see Illustration 7— next page). You don't have to create the channels. They are already there in the Spirit Self. Just watch it happen and receive.

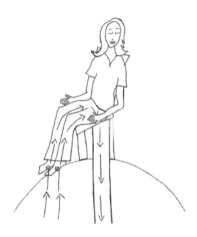

If you haven't already, close your eyes and try it now.

How Does It Feel?

Notice the sensation, texture or flavor of the color you're running. Every color is different for everyone. Is there a word to describe the color you chose? Is it energizing? Relaxing? Peaceful?

If you don't like the color you're running, you can always change it, anytime. To do so, simply stop the color at the center of the Earth. The residual energy will pass through you. Then say "yes" to a brand new color and let it run.

Play with this idea and find an Earth energy color you enjoy. Pick your color, say yes and let your feet chakras call it up. Receive the energy from the center of the Earth into your open feet.

Watch it flow through your leg channels, up past your ankles, into your legs, all the way through to the first chakra. Then let it stream down the grounding cord.

When you've found a color you enjoy, let the Earth energy run on auto-pilot. You don't have to track it.

Now, let's add to this and work with the upper body, and then put the energies together.

The Cosmic Energy Flow

We receive an energy known as "cosmic energy" through the tops of our heads. Some people just don't like the word "cosmic." A good substitute is "Universe" energy, if you'd like an alternative. Here's how it's done:

Re-establish your space if needed (grounding, center of head, bubble and roses). If you've been reading since the beginning of this chapter, you probably already have your tools in place.

Open Your Head

Notice the top of your head. Remember the seventh, or crown, chakra? Picture it as a small circle laying flat on the top of your head. Using the camera shutter or vegetable steamer concept, imagine that circle opening. Let it open to about 60%. Play with it for a moment, opening and closing to find the "just right" spot for you.

Sometimes it seems like a good idea to open the crown way up, but maybe not. Like opening a window in stormy weather, sometimes we don't want to fully open to the surround. For some sensitive folks, a wide open crown invites foreign energy in. How much to open is something you've got to discover for your unique self. If you're not sure, play with 60 or 70%, or simply let go. Trust that your Spirit Self will decide and get it just right.

Open Your Hands

We're also going to open our hands. Would you imagine, in the palm of each hand, a chakra, or opening. See a small circle, camera shutter or tiny vegetable steamer image in the palm of each hand. Open the hand chakras, nice and big, maybe 90% open. Then close them down to just 10%. It is fun to notice that you can tell the difference. This is you becoming more aware of energy.

Play for a moment, and open your hands to a level that feels just right for you; maybe 70 to 80% open. You can always leave it to the Spirit Self to set them just right.

Good job. Now you're ready to receive. Sitting in the middle of your head, would you become aware of the center of the Universe. Every possible color, every possible frequency of energy is available at this point of creation. What color would you like to pick for your cosmic, or Universe, energy? Just like Earth energy, any color except white or black works great.

Why not white or black? I've touched on avoiding white and black for certain exercises back at the beginning with the introduction of the grounding cord. White tends to rev us up, and it tends to attract foreign energy. If you are compelled to use white, try tinting it just a tiny bit to perhaps a light-light blue or light-light yellow, or very light lavender. There are ways to work with white, but it doesn't seem to work well as a color for this particular technique. Black, on the other hand, tends to lure us into unconsciousness, sleepiness and not seeing. If you are drawn to use black, try brown, or a deep blue or slate grey, and see how your body responds.

Where We're Headed

At this point, let me stop and explain the system of channels in the upper body and what we're going to do before we do it. This explanation will make the experience much clearer and smoother when we do take the step.

We'll bring the cosmic energy into two channels at the back of your head. If you were to imagine a clock face laying flat on the top of your head, with 6:00 above your nose, and 12:00 toward the back of your head, these channels would be at about the 11:00 and 1:00 positions of the clock, so at the back of your head and slightly to each side.

Think of the channels like hoses or pipes. They start on the top of your head and flow down the back of your head and neck. At the base of your neck (the back of the fifth chakra energy center), the two channels branch into four, like two rivers dividing and becoming four streams. There are two channels on either side of your spine. How close they are to the center of the back or how far out they are to the sides will be unique to you. With a little practice, you'll be able to see for yourself.

All the channels meet in the first chakra, at the base of your torso, where there grounding cord begins. The cosmic, or Universe, energy will flow into the back of the first chakra and then loop up through the next set of channels, called the front, or core channels.

When I use the word core, I mean center of the body, not just the abdominal area of the body that the word core has come to represent in physical fitness. There are two core, or center, channels. They come up through the first chakra and flow up through your belly, chest, neck and head and end at the top of your head. There is one core channel on either side of the chakras.

Are you saying, "what?" in your head? I know it sounds complicated at first, but bear with me. With just a little practice, the flow will become natural and effortless. You don't have to create the channels, they are already there. So, it's more a process of discovery than hard work.

If you find the vision of the channels just too complex, **simply imagine the energy moving through your body** without the image of the channels. The flow will still happen (see Illustration 8 – next page).

Let It Flow

Let's try running cosmic, or Universe, energy, and then we'll talk about why it's so healing. Here we go:

Check in with your space. In order for this to work, I need you to be grounded. Would you notice that cord. If it's not in place, would you establish grounding. Remember to put the cord on release and bring it to present time.

As you sit in the middle of your head, notice your bubble around you, and your protection roses.

Is your Earth energy still running? If not, invite it up from the center of the Earth. The flow will come right through your bubble and into your open feet chakras, up through your legs, and down the grounding cord. Let it continue to flow without any need to monitor.

Now, notice or imagine the center of the Universe, and remember your cosmic energy color. Invite the flow, say yes, and allow the crown chakra, at the top of your head, to draw the energy towards you.

If you'd like, you could visualize the energy moving through space, past the far-off galaxies and stars, coming closer and closer, reaching our milky way, and our solar system. If that's fun, picture it passing the outer planets and coming into our sky.

Now, see it come down from the sky and flow gently into the back of your head, right into the two channels that are awaiting this wonderful energy. If the space images aren't fun, simply say yes and allow the energy to come to you.

Either way, let the cosmic energy come in and flow through your channels, down the back of your head and neck. Watch with your imagination as the energy flows through the branching where the two channels divide into four. See it flow down your back in all four channels.

Maybe the back muscles relax and the energy flows. Notice how it feels.

Watch what happens when the energy reaches the base of your spine. The channels converge and the energy flows into the back of the first chakra, at the base of your spine.

Next, it loops up, moving into the two core, or center channels; one channel on either side of the chakras. Let that energy flow up through your belly, your chest, your neck, your head, and watch it fountain out the top of your head.

Feel the energy running. Notice the color, and the feel of that color. Earth energy running through your legs and cosmic energy running through your upper body. Breathe.

Two More Steps

You're doing great. Now, let's evolve this process with two more steps. First, notice that as the cosmic energy flows down your back and loops around at the first chakra, it meets the Earth energy in that first chakra.

Imagine the cosmic energy picking up some of that Earth energy before it loops up through your core, so we'll end up with a mixture of all the cosmic energy, plus a bit of the Earth energy, about 10 or 15% of it, coming up through the core.

Let this begin to happen now. Imagine Earth energy coming up from the center of the Earth and flowing through your leg channels, to the grounding cord, and back down to the center of the Earth. Envision cosmic energy coming into the back of your head into two channels. Watch the branching to four channels, two on either side of your spine, and flowing down your back.

As the cosmic energy comes into the back of the first chakra, watch it to mix with the Earth energy. Bring the mixture of all that cosmic energy plus about 10 or 15% of the Earth energy up through the two channels that run along either side of the chakras. Let it flow up through your belly, chest, neck and head. Watch the mixture fountain out the top of your head.

Some people like to allow a portion of the cosmic energy to go down the grounding cord too, about 10 or 15%. That feels more balanced to them. I like to bring all that cosmic energy up through the core. Try it both ways and, as you play, you'll discover what's best for you.

As the Earth and cosmic mixture flow up through you, see the energy fountain out the top of your head. Watch it effervesce through your aura, showering you in a flow of light and cleansing the energy field around you. Eventually, it will find its way down the grounding cord.

Almost There!

Fantastic job! There's just one more piece to this process. I know, I know – it is a lot. Take it one step at a time and you'll have it down before you know it. And, I'll summarize all the steps at the end of this chapter in a quick reference.

Remember, if you find the vision of the channels just too complex, simply imagine the energy moving through your body without the image of the channels. The flow will still happen.

Now, back to running energy. As that mixture flows up through you, let's let some of it, just a bit, flow down each of your arms. That flow into the arms will begin at the base of your throat, the fifth chakra. Let this happen now.

As the energy flows up the two core channels, when it reaches the base of your neck, watch some of it, maybe 10% on each side, branch away from the main flow. See it flow across your shoulders, down your arms and out your open hand chakras.

You've become an energy fountain (see Illustration 8). Energy is moving into you through your feet and through your head, and energy is flowing out of you through your first chakra, head and hands. Take a moment to enjoy the sensation of flow, cleansing from the inside out.

Once you have it set up, you don't have to track the flow. It simply happens. Monitoring it can get annoying and distracting. Instead, let the flow continue, like turning on a faucet. Once the water is running through the pipes, it will continue to run.

How It Works

Now that we've done it, let's talk about why running energy is so important to our waking up, staying awake and living to our highest.

Running Earth and cosmic energy clears the chakras. The center, or core, channels connect with the chakras as they flow. The chakras spin, and can release energy into the channels where it will be flushed out. Remember from Chapter Four; the chakras are libraries of information. Flowing energy helps clear the chakras of books we've read and don't want to re-read. That information might be experienced as old patterns, limiting beliefs, physical pain or a myriad of other forms.

In short, we're clearing anything that doesn't serve our best experience of ourselves and our lives. We're making space for our present time energy and creating the opportunity to change our realities. That's amazing!

You may begin to feel groggy, tired or irritated as the cleansing happens. If so, please keep going. It's very likely a chakra is releasing, and you are experiencing the energy as it surfaces. If you'll keep running energy, it will clear quickly and the sensation will pass. Don't stop in mid-cleanse, leaving the energy at the surface without clearing it.

A Way to Step It Up

If you'd like, you can accelerate the chakra cleansing by adding in some addition Meditation for Living skills to the process. You could create energy containers, fill them with energy to be released and let it go by destroying the container. Remember how we did this in Chapter 3? Here's a quick review:

• Imagine in front of you, out in your energy field, or aura, a container into which you will release this energy. The container could be a bubble, balloon, trash bag or anything you can imagine.
• Write the name of the vibration you'd like to release on the container, labeling it. Or, simply label it "energy I don't need."
• Allow the vibration you're releasing to move from your body, charkas and energy field into the container.

• When the container is full, imagine tossing it high into the sky. Imagine destroying the container by blowing it up, disintegrating it, or however you'd like to extinguish this symbol. The energy is now released and transmuted.
• Notice what vibration you would like to experience instead of the one you just let go of.
• Bring in a gold sun of any vibration you'd like.

You can do this while energy is running. It's not hard at all once you get used to the flow. And, it will only take a minute or two to clear what's been stuck in that chakra, perhaps for years. With flowing energy, always stop on a high note when you're feeling good.

Have You Tried It Yet?

If you haven't, close your eyes and walk through the steps. It may help to re-read a section, try it, and then add the next step, and so on.

When you've got the energy flowing, try creating and destroying as it runs. Imagine a balloon in front of you, or whatever kind of container you'd like, and notice a vibration you'd like to let go of in your life; maybe struggle, stress, worry or any vibration you'd like to release. Imagine releasing the vibration into the container, and then toss the container away, high into the sky, and burst or destroy it.

Now give yourself a big gold sun. You can bring in a gold sun while the Earth and cosmic energy are running. It won't disrupt the flow at all. Create a big gold sun above your head, write across that sun a word that represents the energy you'd like to receive, watch the sun absorb the word and fill yourself in.

Play with this meditation as long as you'd like, or as long as fits in your schedule, always stopping on a high note and not in the middle of an uncomfortable release.

A Reminder to Take It Easy

Remember at the beginning of the session, when I said that this process is usually challenging at first? If you are confused, that's ok. Let yourself just play with the concept of the channels and the flow. With a little practice, you'll love how it feels.

The cleansing provided by flowing Earth and cosmic energies is irreplaceable, and will make an immediate and significant difference in your life. Plus, once you're familiar with the process, it feels great and so relaxing.

With the running of Earth and cosmic energy, we've added an amazing power tool to our toolbox of meditation skills. From this point forward, we'll use these skills to go even deeper into meditation, relaxation, conscious change and healing.

Running Energy In A Nutshell

The steps below summarize the running energy process:

• Earth Energy First
   o Notice and open the feet chakras.
   o Notice the center of the Earth.
   o Pick the Earth energy color your body would like to run (not white or black).

o Let the color run; up from the center of the Earth, into your open feet chakras, through the leg channels and down the grounding cord.

- Cosmic Energy:
    o Notice and open the hand chakras.
    o Notice and open the crown (seventh) chakra at the top of your head.
    o Notice the center of the Universe.
    o Pick the cosmic energy color your body would like to run (not white or black).
    o Let the color run.
    o From the Center of the Universe into your crown chakra; into two channels down the back of your head and neck.
    o At the base of your neck (5th chakra) the two channels branch into four (two on either side of your spine).
    o Let the channels fill and the energy flow down your back.
    o The channels converge, and Earth and cosmic energies meet in the first chakra (base of your spine).
    o Watch the Earth and cosmic energies mix.
    o Bring the mixture of all the cosmic energy, plus about 10 or 15% of the Earth energy up through the "front," or center channels. There is one channel on either side of the chakras, and the channels touch the chakras, and help them cleanse.
    o Let the energy fountain out the top of your head.
    o As energy flows up through the "front"/center channels, allow some of it (10% or so each side) to flow across your shoulders, down your arms and out your open hand chakras.

Enjoy the flow!

Reminders:

Once the energies are running, you do not need to track them. You could check in with them, but you don't need to monitor. Your body will naturally allow the energy to run.

And, if working with the channels is too complex for you, simply imagine the energy moving through your body without the image of the channels.

EXPERIENCING SPIRITUAL AWARENESS

CHAPTER 6 : PUTTING IT ALL TOGETHER

With the inclusion of running energy, we've reached a milestone in the journey. You now have all the basic concepts, the tools, for waking up to yourself as spirit and bridging the communication gap between your Human Self and Spirit Self.

Your toolbox is brimming with grounding, center of head, your aura bubble and roses, running energy, creating and destroying and gold suns. You have all the basics you need for living spiritually awake, and for waking up should you doze off again. In Part 2, we'll talk about applying the tools to build your life of joy and abundance.

First, let's savor the moment with a full review of the skills and some tips on how to use them. Below is step-by-step outline of how to find your space, the process of coming home to yourself and letting go of the illusion of daily life.

You'll notice that I've listed running energy before establishing your aura bubble and protection roses. Even though I teach the aura bubble before running energy, in practice I get my energy running before establishing the bubble. I've found that it's much easier for people to learn the other way around, so I present it in the order you've experienced so far. Walk through the steps in whatever order feels right to you. I do request you try it my way at least a couple of times before deciding. (Thanks!)

Steps to Finding Your Space

Step 1: Grounding
• Imagine a grounding cord extending from your first chakra energy center at the base of your spine.
• Watch the cord grow all the way to the center of the Earth and connect it there using whatever image you like to represent the Earth's core.
• Add the power switch, putting the grounding cord on release, powering the grounding cord to help you let go.
• Last, add the present time date, inviting yourself right into the moment.

Step 2: Center of Head / Sixth Chakra
• Gather your focus, or point of attention, in the center of your head. Imagine walking into your center of head room.
• Change at least one thing about the room to freshen your awareness of it and bring it to present time.
• Settle in to your center of head room, with the intention of staying there even as you become aware of the other aspects of your space.
• Clear your center of head of others' energies

Step 3: Run Your Energy
• Notice and open the feet chakras.
• Notice the center of the Earth.

- Pick the Earth energy color your body would like to run (not white or black).
- Let the color run up from the center of the Earth into your open feet chakras, through the leg channels and down the grounding cord.
- Notice and open the hand chakras.
- Notice and open the crown (seventh) chakra at the top of your head.
- Notice the center of the Universe.
- Pick the cosmic energy color your body would like to run (not white or black).
- Let the color run.
- From the Center of the Universe into your crown chakra; into two channels down the back of your head and neck.
- At the base of your neck (5th chakra) the two channels branch into four (two on either side of your spine).
- Let the channels fill and the energy flow down your back.
- The channels converge, and Earth and cosmic energies meet in the first chakra (base of your spine).
- Watch the Earth and cosmic energies mix.
- Bring the mixture of all the cosmic energy, plus about 10 or 15% of the Earth energy up through the "front," or center channels. There is one channel on either side of the chakras. The channels touch the chakras.
- Let the energy fountain out the top of your head.
- As energy flows up through the "front"/center channels, allow some of it (10% or so each side) to flow across your shoulders, down your arms and out your open hand chakras.

Step 4: Set Up Your Aura Bubble and Protection Roses

- Check for old protection roses around you. Cut their stems, let the excess stems fall to the center of the Earth and destroy the old roses.
- Create a brand new rose in front of you.
- Send the rose to find the furthest away place your energy is scattered (a physical place, another person's space, or a point in time).
- Call the rose home.
- Notice the bubble form around you as the rose gets closer.
- When the rose reaches a distance of about an arm's length in front of you, extend its stem to the center of the Earth, grounding it.
- Set up the five other roses at the five additional delineation points around the aura; the back, right side, left side, top and bottom of the bubble.

All At Once or On the Fly

The skills come together to create an effective, relaxing and life-affirming meditation practice. And, they can be used to quickly change your space without going through the whole process. For example, you could ground and bring in a gold sun anytime. Or, ground and create and destroy roses or other containers for releasing energy.

Standing in line at a store, being stopped at a red light, waiting on hold on the phone and taking a break in the restroom are all good examples of opportunities to pull out a tool or two. **You can play with your tools in any way you'd like, as long as you ground first.** Without grounding, the other concepts become much less effective.

For Best Results

People often inquire about when the best time of day is for meditation. And, they wonder how long they should meditate. The answer to both is, "whatever works in your life."

Ideally, you'll find fifteen minutes or so in your day to find your space and meditate. As we continue on the journey and your awareness grows, you might want more time to engage your awareness in focused ways using the concepts to come.

It's best to practice sitting in a chair in a quiet space for some piece of time with reasonable frequency. I've played tennis on and off over the years. Attending the drills and practicing the strokes until they become natural helps me play the game with more ease and fun. The tools are much the same way. If you take the time to practice with them, you'll find you can pull out the tools in times of challenge with ease.

I like to meditate up to an hour a day, but let's be real. An hour is an unrealistic goal for most, and can be a set up for failure. Don't create an unreasonable expectation for yourself. Instead, notice that even five minutes, even two minutes, is much more than none. Just grounding changes the moment, and maybe even the rest of your day.

Look at your life. Where is your fifteen minutes? Where does meditation fit in? If you hit the ground running in the morning with work, kids or both, that's probably not the time for you. Pick a time; perhaps at lunch, at the end of the day or at mid-morning break and begin.

Lose Your Space ~ Get It Back

You'll notice that, once you set up your tools, they don't last forever. You could easily lose your grounding cord during a confrontation or challenging situation. You may find your protection roses damaged or missing after a rough day.

The idea is not to hold your space perpetually. You can lose your space. That's not a problem because you can simply get it back by reestablishing your tools. It happens all the time.

What Now?

Once you are in your space, the world of energy is yours to explore. You could release energies you'd like to let go of and replace them with gold suns of vibrations you'd prefer. Or, you could simply relax and enjoy the flow, knowing that the energy running through you is clearing. Your meditation practice will reward you with a more empowered and joyful life.

In upcoming chapters, we'll expand our practice to more skillfully dance with the possibilities of reality and to inventory, change and create our own Universe of experience.

Now that you're awake, there's a big party to go to: your own life.

PART 2: LIVING SPIRITUAL AWARENESS

INTRODUCTION:
THE MIRACLE OF THE DIMES

In the spring of the year 2000, a group of fellow seekers and I went on a retreat in Hawaii with a wonderful spiritual teacher, Michael Tamura. The process involved practicing meditation and clairvoyance for up to eight hours a day, followed by the delicious delights of the big island.

One night we all went to the hotel lounge. The waiter brought a drink for me offered by a man at the bar, a fruity daiquiri, umbrella and all. I accepted and decided to cut loose. I can't remember his name, but I do remember his cute blonde hair and tanned skin. We danced the night away at several local hotspots and kissed on the beach. The next day, I felt awful.

Hung over and tired, I forced myself to get up and attend the morning meditation. At the lunch break, three friends and I cut out. Behaving badly, we went to a fast food joint and took our lunches back to the hotel.

After enjoying a greasy burger and large fries, I sat on the bed, my belly full and my body exhausted. I lay back, dangling my feet over the edge of the bed. I closed my eyes and dozed, listening to the comforting chatter of friends.

Suddenly, I felt little pings on the tops and in the arches of my feet, just like raindrops. I sat up and looked at my feet. There was a dime on the top of my right foot and one under each foot. I went perfectly still and called to the other women.

After about twenty minutes of counting everyone's change and trying to figure it out, we allowed ourselves to realize that the dimes had manifested from my feet; an expression of spiritual creation. Celebration ensued with jumping on beds and joyous tears for the possibilities of reality.

I am blessed by this event in many ways, by far the most important being that it happened when I wasn't doing the "right thing." I felt so guilty about drinking too much, staying out all night and missing the afternoon lessons. The miracle of the dimes showed me that only I created the guilt.

The message was crystal clear. My Spirit Self isn't judging, nor is the consciousness that creates this Universe. It was a life-changing event for me, and I treasure those dimes to this day as a reminder of this priceless information.

We live in a time when metaphysical philosophies and spiritual paradigms are quickly gaining ground. It's a wonderful transition away from the mythological stories and punishment/reward systems of traditional religions. Still, that toxic energy can creep into even the metaphysical consciousness.

The idea of intending just right, relentlessly monitoring one's thoughts, speaking just right, eating just right or living just right "or else" is out there even now. It's a metaphysical religion.

I invite you to step away from this and into the awareness that all judgment is optional.

Punishment and reward, right and wrong are simplistic, constricting concepts that limit the possibilities of reality. We choose and get a result. Punishment happens when we hold the result against ourselves instead of allowing wisdom from experience.

You are a magnificent, unique part of the whole. Each of us is an irreplaceable ray of the same sun. Once again, in the larger perspective of Spirit, you just can't get it wrong. As we move forward, please keep this in mind with a tenderness toward yourself as you grow, unfold and become aware of the beauty that you are.

LIVING SPIRITUAL AWARENESS

CHAPTER 1: THE TRANSITION

In this leg of our journey, we'll use the skills you've acquired in Part 1 to explore your Universe of reality. Life happens through us, not to us. So, we can change our experience by changing our inner landscape of energy.

It's simple, but not always easy. Along the way, pain may surface. Pain is caused by energy that doesn't resonate with your Spirit Self. The hurt is the symptom, not the problem. Discomfort is a great way to get our attention, for the Spirit Self to say, "Hey, this doesn't belong."

Pain can be an indication of a belief that doesn't fit with your natural information; a repressed, old emotion or highly-charged memory; someone else's energy or information in your space. Pain can be physical, mental or emotional. Whatever the form, pain is a manifestation of energy that's not in harmony with who you really are.

Pain Is Information

Allowing discomfort is a spiritual skill. If you experience emotional upset, confusion or sorrow along the path of inventorying your personal reality, let it come. Say hello to it, and listen. Notice what the pain is saying, instead of pushing it down again. It's come to be transformed into wisdom by the light of awareness. Pain will show you what's not your path and what to release.

I'm presenting a gentle warning here, picturing myself like a forest ranger at one of the trailheads in beautiful Yellowstone Park. "Watch out for snakes, bears and unstable ground. Bring plenty of water." On the trail, while there are potential challenges, most of the walk is beautiful and refreshing.

So it is with the journey of spiritual awareness. Old "stuff," painful memories or uncomfortable vibrations may arise. If so, we'll work with them to release the old and create a life that's a reflection of who and what you really are.

Most of the journey is adventurous and fun. And the view of life and yourself from the peak of true awareness is spectacular!

Let's add a few more concepts to your supplies to make the trek more comfortable.

Havingness

Havingness is a vibration; like love, peace, fear or joy. Havingness involves allowing, receiving and deserving. On one level, we could think of havingness in terms of material gain or loss. If someone wins the lottery and then loses it all in the first year, we could say they couldn't "have" it. Their picture of themselves couldn't expand to include massive wealth.

If someone claims to want a relationship, but continually finds fault with every potential partner, maybe they can't have being in the relationship, but they can have wanting it.

Havingness reflects how we see ourselves, and our capacity for ranges of reality. I'm introducing a brand new word to describe a very important energy. Increasing havingness in our space broadens our possibilities of experience. When we expand the range of potential realities we can embrace, we grow beyond old limitations and beliefs more easily.

Think of havingness as spherical, rather than linear. It doesn't expand in just one direction. One of my favorite havingness experiences happened in the early days of the Inner Connection Institute, the outreach arm of our spiritual organization.

We were operating out of a small house in downtown Denver. One of the students was a beautiful but timid woman I'll call Lucy. One day Lucy told me she was in an abusive relationship and was going to leave her husband She wanted me to know that sometime within the next few weeks, she would stop showing up for class and not to worry about her.

Sure enough, three weeks later, Lucy disappeared. Several days later a man came to the door while I was at the house alone. I answered to discover it was Lucy's husband, and he was mad. He thought I had convinced Lucy to leave, and that I knew where she was. As he stood on the other side of the screen door yelling and gesturing, I grounded myself.

I felt oddly at peace with the situation and realized what was happening. **I could "have" this man be angry with me.** I could allow this reality. There was a time in my life where, had that happened, fear would have driven me to close not only the door, but the business, deciding to validate a reality based on fear.

Instead, I could have the moment. I smiled as I realized that, my reality of fear had dissolved. The encounter was a beautiful reflection of my growth. And, even more, if I could have this event, havingness would expand in all directions, and my sense of safety would allow many more students to come to the door.

My serenity disarmed Lucy's husband. He stopped ranting and asked, "Do you know where she is?" I replied that I didn't, and that I was glad I didn't, so that I had no inner conflict about not sharing any information.

This startled him so that he went silent and walked away. I closed the door and thanked God and myself that I had released old fears, and that the door to the Inner Connection Institute was truly wide open.

My havingness had expanded to allow the experience, and since havingness is spherical, it also expanded to include a much larger student population of lovely, graceful seekers.

Now, increasing your own havingness doesn't mean you're going to have an angry man at your door! I share this just to illustrate the expansive nature of havingness. Just because you can have it, doesn't mean you must experience it.

Bringing up your havingness will allow more into your reality. As we decide what's true and safe along our journey of life, we narrow our range of possible realities. Havingness opens things up.

Increasing havingness is simple. Just bring it in with the gold sun tool. If you want more havingness, bring in gold suns of it. While grounded, simply create a gold sun over your head, write the word 'havingness' across it, watch the sun become that vibration and then pop it. Fill in each chakra, your whole body, and your aura bubble with this amazing vibration.

Notice the texture or energetic flavor of havingness as you receive. If you enjoy it, I'd suggest you bring in several gold suns of havingness each day for a week or two. Notice how you, and your world, begin to shift toward greater abundance.

Amusement

Amusement, a powerful force of lightness, is another great vibration to bring along on the path of spiritual growth. Laughter brings perspective and lightness. Spiritual amusement is never at anyone's expense. Rather, it gives us a wonderful perspective on the journey of life, and reminds us to take a step back, or really a step up, when we take ourselves and life too seriously.

Think of the Dalai Lama, a man of tremendous peace and wisdom. He's got a great humor about him - that's spiritual amusement.

Just like havingness, you can increase amusement by filling in with gold suns of this vibration. Try it now. Do you notice the difference between havingness and amusement? They are different, but like peanut butter and chocolate, they go great together.

Present Time

One last piece to carry along on the journey is the concept of present time. In the here and now, anything is possible. Truly being in present time requires a special level of letting go.

If we consider that the energies we carry create our reality, the idea of past experience transforms. Often we make decisions about what's true based on events that occurred along our timeline. That seems to make sense.

But if life happens through us, history doesn't show us what's true; it shows us what energies we were carrying at the time of the experience. This concept is key in reframing our timelines and becoming free of our histories. I call it the Myth of Past Experience.

In our early years, we didn't have a choice about the energies we carried. We had them bestowed upon us by family and culture. We were asleep, deep in the throes of spiritual amnesia, so we took it all on. Once we wake up, we can make a change.

The dysfunctional relationships with men I created in my early adulthood were an expression of the wounding I carried from unhealthy family dynamics. They were a brilliant expression of the core beliefs I carried about my worth and value. If I were to use them to define present time, I'd never date again!

Once I could see the invalidation and wounding and heal it, I could create differently. I changed the energy and set the stage for a new experience.

Most of what controls us isn't happening in present time. So, **in present time, we can release and be free.** As you explore yourself, be in present time. Let go of the Myth of Past Experience and move into the truth of now.

Taking the Next Step

Havingness and amusement lighten the load along the journey of spiritual growth and make any rough spots much easier to navigate. Being in present time empowers you to see what's old and let it go.

With these concepts, coupled with your meditation skills, you're well-prepared for the scenery ahead. You're ready to go.

LIVING SPIRITUAL AWARENESS

CHAPTER 2: INTENTION AND MANIFESTATION

Intention and Manifestation are important concepts to consider as we look at creating our own reality more purposefully. When we reconnect the Human Self and Spirit Self, we become more powerful. It's important to wield these abilities with wisdom.

Intention is the energetic concept, thought form or idea. Manifestation is the bringing forth of that concept into actual experience.

We're all doing it all the time without any deliberate focus. **We're walking around creating our lives without even thinking about it.** Conscious manifestation is a highly underused ability.

We're going to be intending and manifesting with awareness. The first consideration is, of course, "what do I really want?"

True spiritual desire is a message from our Spirit Self to help direct us on our path. Genuine desire of the heart is like a neon sign reading "Your Path This Way." Follow the directions your yearning points to and you follow your highest path.

As you be who you really are and express that authenticity through your life, you bring your unique gifts into expression. These gifts are your contributions that are needed by yourself and others on Earth.

Now, let me be clear that I'm referring to the true, deep desire that lives in your hearts. I'm not talking about wanting to change yourself based on self-judgment or desires that help you escape pain. If you are thinking that your true spiritual desire is to be slim and trim, we're not on the same page.

I'm talking about the true intentions of you as a soul incarnated; what the Spirit Self knows you are meant to do and be in this life.

These desires sometimes have a "but" right after them. For example, someone saying, "I'd like to join a chorus, but I'm not good enough." Or, "I'd like to open an animal rescue, but I don't have the resources." Even, "I'd like to start my own business, but I'm afraid."

As you use your Meditation for Living tools, you'll likely notice true desire come to the surface. And, you'll more easily recognize the desires that are based on self-judgment or pain, and let those go, as you move into self-awareness and self-love.

You will increase your capacity to bring forth your dreams, and you can release the buts, the fears and any other energy that blocks your creativity.

Pizza as a Spiritual Consideration

Sometimes true desire seems small, but it is always significant. At one point in the journey, I worked with a healer named Don. Don is doing amazing things communicating with blood to obtain information and inserting electrical codes to re-set vibrations in the body. And, he sets the energy of water like medicine. He literally brought my cat back from the brink of death by remotely working on her through a blood sample. Wow!

I first met with Don in hopes of taking a step with food allergies. Throughout my young adulthood, I had tremendous difficulty with digestion. Eventually, I took a food allergy blood test to find I was allergic to over 50 foods! After a brutal detoxification diet, it all came down to dairy, eggs and corn. I spent over ten years abstaining from them. Then, at age 40, I heard about Don.

Knowing about my work, Don asked me my spiritual goal for working with him. I stated with absolute certainty, "I'd like to eat pizza again in this lifetime." He laughed and laughed. We began a course of healing.

In the sessions, I communicated with my body about being free in present time as he engaged with my blood and reprogrammed my body. I took my water with gratitude each day.

I'm happy to share that I now enjoy pizza about once a week. I savor every bite of melted cheese like a gift from the gods. My food allergies are no longer an issue.

Although enjoying pizza is a big part of this healing, it symbolizes much more for me. My spiritual desire to enjoy the bounty of the planet reflects a freedom within.

In my childhood, I'd been told over and over that my sensitivity was a problem. Then, my parents referred to my energetic sensitivity, my seeing and speaking what I saw. I'd been programmed that I didn't fit in, that I was too different.

That energy was expressing in the food sensitivities, as if I wasn't the same as everyone else. It was on my path to release that energy and be both sensitive and a part of it all. **My sensitivity isn't a problem at all; it's my greatest gift.**

What About You?

As you close the gap between your Human Self and Spirit Self, let yourself begin to wonder what you'd really like for your life. You don't have to know right away, just wondering or asking opens doors to awareness.

Perhaps the reality you've created isn't reflective of who you really are in one or more areas. Does your work reflect your genuine passion? Does your intimate relationship reflect your true self-worth?

When you notice something you want to manifest, try this meditation to work with yourself and the Universe to bring it into physical reality. You can think big or think small. It's a matter of havingness, as you'll see below.

This technique can be used for any intention; acquiring something material, a shift in a situation or a shift in your own vibration. I'd suggest reading through the whole process first, then try it step-by-step.

Mocking-Up

In this meditation, we'll create what's called a mock-up. The term comes from the architectural field. A mock-up is a small representation of a building or structure to come. It's a perfect metaphor for what we'll be doing. We'll be creating an energetic symbol of what you'd like to see manifest in reality.

This process engages your Human Self, your Spirit Self and the energy of the all-one consciousness to affect reality. I'll walk you through it, with lots of description and comments along the way. At the end of this Chapter, there's a step-by-step summary of the process.

First, start out by meditating. Walk through the steps outlined in Chapter 6 of Part 1. It's important to be in your space and connected with your Spirit Self as you work with this technique.

As you sit with yourself in the powerful meditative stance of consciousness, become aware of something you'd like to manifest in your life. If it's your first time, you might want to try something rather simple; like finding something you've been looking for, or you practicing meditation regularly or someone buying you lunch.

You might want to think bigger; perhaps the resolution of a particular conflict or challenge, maybe a particular job or contract, perhaps a relationship or you in a particular condition (perhaps you feeling joyous, and at peace).

A quick aside here: it's not a good idea to mock-up for another person. You don't know their path, and it's just too tempting to imagine we know what's good for someone else. If you're tempted, instead simply see them as a powerful soul; creating, learning, growing in their own way and time and free to change patterns whenever it's time.

Notice something you'd like to create for yourself.

Now, imagine a rose in front of you. This is a brand new rose, distinct from your protection roses around you. Notice if you like this rose and want to work with it for this exercise. If not, toss it away, blow it up or destroy it however you like to destroy, and create another one.

Next, imagine a picture, just like a photo, next to the rose. The picture is of the desire fulfilled. It's you holding the object you've been looking for, it's you practicing your meditation, it's you eating that free meal or you working at that new job.

Contemplate the image for a moment. Confirm that the picture is of fruition, not of wanting. If you mock-up wanting something, then that is what you'll manifest, wanting it.

Clear Chatter and Doubt

As you sit with this picture, if there are reasons that come up in your thoughts about why it can't happen or you fall into mind chatter, simply re-find the center of your head. Then, create a bubble or balloon off to the side in you in your aura and let the reasons flow into it, all those critical thoughts and any doubt. Imagine putting it all in a bubble or balloon (it may take more than one). Then, you know what to do: let it go. Toss that bubble or balloon full of reasons and doubt away and burst it, freeing yourself of those distractions.

Some of those reasons may have focused on how this intention can come to be. When mocking-up, don't concern yourself with how the process might unfold. Give your Spirit Self space to be creative. When we get out of the way, surprising steps that we may never have thought of often transpire.

When you trust that this intention can come through, without needing to know how it will happen, imagine sliding the picture right into the flower part of the rose. Watch the rose absorb the picture. It may shimmer, perk up or somehow respond to the energy. It's now a "mock-up rose."

Next, ground the rose, extending its stem all the way to the center of the Earth. This allows any residual negativity to ground off.

Two Optional Steps

At this point, we could get more specific. But it's a little tricky. Putting too much form on a mock-up can limit possibilities. If there are specifics, this is the time to put them in. You could insert them as words, thoughts or images. For example, if you are manifesting the perfect new coat for you, and it has to be green, you could put that thought in there; it's green. However, I always caution against too much form.

If you are mocking up a job, I'd suggest picturing you working at the perfect job for you; happy, prosperous and fulfilled. That leaves the Universe a lot more room to play than if you mock-up a particular job at a specific place. Do it in whatever way feels right to you, but please do keep this concept in mind.

We could also create a timeline. Again this is a tricky one. I always set my mock-ups at divine timing. I never put calendar time on them. If you'd like to intend a time schedule, simply imagine a line above the rose; a simple line to represent time, with the beginning of the timeline at present time and the end of the timeline at manifestation and imagine the length of the timeline at the duration you'd like.

Please be flexible with the concept of time. Sometimes what we think we'd like on a personality level isn't in sync with our soul's timing.

When you're ready, drop the timeline into the mock-up rose and watch the rose absorb it.

If you'd like to set the mock-up at divine timing, simply put the thought; Thank you Spirit, Universe, God or whatever word you like; Thank you Universe, that this mock-up is manifest in divine timing.

Fill 'Er Up

Now, let's fill this mock-up with some vibrations. Inserting energies like fun, clarity or ease helps mock-ups flow. To put a vibration in the mock-up, imagine a small gold sun floating above the rose. Put a word in it, perhaps fun, clarity, ease or whatever you'd like. Watch the sun absorb the word and set it right into the rose. Put in as many vibrations as you'd like. I have a friend who always puts in "cooler than I can imagine" at the end. Maybe you'd like that.

Check Your Havingness

Good job. You're sitting in meditation, looking at your mock-up rose. Do you know in your heart that you can have this? Is your level of havingness such that you can really see yourself in this manifestation and know it can be so, even if you don't know how it will happen?

If not, give yourself some gold suns of havingness right now. Raise your havingness, your capacity for possibilities, your capacity for how you see yourself, until you really know you deserve this in your life and can receive it.

If you look at the rose and know you cannot have it, if you just don't believe it, it might be a good idea to let it go. Destroy this mock-up rose, and do your work in meditation over the next few days or weeks to raise your sense of yourself and release doubt to the point where you can have it. Then, revisit creating with this technique.

Let It Go

So, here you are, looking at your mock-up rose. Would you top it off with one more gold sun, one of havingness?

We're going to let this mock-up go out into the Universe. Letting the mock-up go is like placing your order at a restaurant. You communicate your desire and trust that it will come to you. You don't follow the waiter back to the kitchen and watch the cook prepare it.

To let the mock-up go, first cut the stem of the rose at some distance from the flower part, leaving some stem with the flower, and letting the rest fall to the center of the Earth. Next, imagine putting the rose inside a big balloon. Mock-up balloons tend to work well at either gold or pink in color.

Now, release it. Watch the mock-up go off into the Universe. Do NOT blow it up. Leave it intact, and trust. Know that this intention will come back to you in physical form, in divine timing. In this case, the waiter and cook are you as Spirit Self, co-creating with God, Spirit or whatever word you like for the consciousness that creates this Universe; mixing ingredients in harmony with the unfolding of reality in divine timing.

Spirit Says Yes

God is a highly charged word for some. When I refer to God, I mean the consciousness that creates this Universe. I see that consciousness always vibrating at yes. Yes to whatever we believe. I am happy – YES. I am prosperous – YES. I am troubled – YES. I am not good enough – YES. We create reality from the inside out. **What we believe, think and say to ourselves is important beyond measure.**

When working with the concept of the consciousness that creates this Universe, use whatever word you like; God, Spirit, Universe, Energy, All-One or whatever is comfortable for you. The consciousness will know what you mean.

Tips for Mocking-Up

Here are a few suggestions about using mock-ups in your journey of life.

If you've mocked something up, and then want to do it again, call back the old mock-up and destroy it. Simply imagine the old balloon coming back, rose inside, and destroy it. Then, create the mock-up brand new. Mocking-up the same thing over and over in slightly different ways disperses the force of creation across different forms. So, clean the old one out of your reality before creating the new.

Also, watch that your mock-ups are in harmony with each other and not in conflict. For example, if you mock-up you working at Apple and you mock-up you working at Microsoft, those are distinctly different energies. Think of ordering a steak and an ice cream sundae to arrive at your table at the same time. They're both wonderful experiences, but not at the same time. Pick one for now, or, even better, simply loosen the form. In this example that would mean mocking-up you working at the perfect job for you; happy, prosperous, fulfilled and surrounded by people with whom you enjoy spending your day.

And, poking at a mock-up doesn't help it happen. There's no need to check in with it over and over again. Instead, if you want to support the manifestation without over-checking it, simply affirm, whenever you'd like: Thank you God (or Spirit or Universe of whatever word suits you) that this mock-up is manifested in divining timing. Also, it helps for you to frequently clean out any energies and old beliefs in you that would block the manifestation; like doubt, resistance, mistrust or uncertainty, and fill yourself with havingness instead.

Ultimately, the journey of any mock-up is a journey of self discovery and personal growth. The path leads from how we see ourselves today to how we see ourselves in that manifestation. That may require letting go of what stands between how we see ourselves without the creation and how we see ourselves with the mock-up manifested.

And, last, you will have to show up to the process! If you mock-up you working at the perfect job for you and simply sit at home on your couch all day, it's not likely to manifest. You need to be out in the world doing your part. You wouldn't expect a pizza to arrive on your table without picking up the phone to order it and then answering the doorbell. Hmmmm – pizza!

A Deeper Look at Desire

Why do we want what we want? As I've mentioned, spiritual yearning is a signpost of one's path. Also, true desire invokes growth. The manifestation of a vision stretches our havingness for how we see ourselves; what we know we can be, do and receive. We break through limiting beliefs through the creative process.

Often we think we want something because we believe it will bring us a particular internal condition. We may want money because we believe it will bring a feeling of security or peace. Maybe a new outfit will bring self-confidence.

It's always about the vibration, not the thing. In considering your desires, ask yourself how you believe you'll feel when you receive them. Loved? At peace? Happy? It's the energetic frequency that will bring the feeling, and you can have that right now. Become an attractor instead of a seeker by bringing in gold suns of the energies you'd expect to feel on manifestation. Have those vibrations now, and you'll attract more of the same.

Becoming what you seek is a transformative experience. You'll see that you really do create your experience and that reality happens from the inside out.

With these concepts in mind, I hope you'll enjoy bringing the mock-up process into your meditations and your life. Below is a step-by-step summary of the process:

Step-By-Step Creation
- Imagine a rose in front of you.
- Imagine a picture, just like a photo, next to the rose.
- Confirm that the image is of fulfillment and not of wanting.
- Clean out reasons it can't happen.
- Clean out doubt.
- Slide the picture into the flower part of the rose.
- Ground the rose by extending its stem all the way to the center of the Earth.
- Put in any specifics. Be mindful to keep the form as loose as possible.
- Put in the timeline, or the intention of divine timing.
- Fill the rose with vibrations you'd like in the experience.
- Check your havingness.
  - o If havingness is low, raise it or consider revisiting this creation when you've raised havingness.
- Give the mock-up rose a gold sun of havingness.
- Let it go.

LIVING SPIRITUAL AWARENESS

CHAPTER 3: DECISION POINTS

Since reality happens through us and not to us, we get what we believe. Believing is seeing. Often we don't realize what we believe; we just feel as if we know what's true and real. We get used to seeing ourselves and the world in a particular way. But do we really know what's real, or are we just used to believing something is true? Most all decisions about reality are fluid, even when it doesn't seem that way.

Along the journey of life, there are decision points when we make choices about what's true. Once we make a decision, we run our reality through it like a filter. The filter narrows what we can see, believe and create.

Decision Points as Pictures

In the Spirit Self, these decision points appear as pictures in the aura or chakras. Pictures can be released and decisions can be changed.

Some pictures are helpful to manifesting a joyful reality and some aren't. For instance, I have a friend who has made a reality decision that "money is never a problem." And in her life, it isn't. Yet, a woman I know casually from a place I go to get massages often talks about being "broke" or just "on the edge" and so that is what she is experiencing.

These are two capable, lovely women living in the same city at the same time. They are both getting what they believe.

We're each carrying a photo album within us, each picture representing a decision point. The collection could be titled, "My Story of What's True." And, my story will dictate my present time possibilities of experience. Isn't it extraordinary that we can re-write the story? We can, in effect, change the past by changing the influence it has on us now. What power!

Where Do Pictures Come From?

We acquire pictures in a number of ways. First, we create them through our life experiences. When I was a junior in high school, I went to visit my then-boyfriend at college. During the weekend, I realized he was dating another young woman. She was super skinny, and I mean a stick figure.

I decided at that point that I would be more loveable if I were really thin. That took some doing, because my body just isn't naturally that way. I kept that up for a couple of years and then released the decision, or destroyed the picture.

During my time of self-healing (which really never ends), I traced that decision to a moment. It looked just like a photograph in my second chakra. A group of young people walking down a Philadelphia side street on the way to a local bar, my vision falling on my boyfriend with the slender woman walking beside him. They weren't touching, but all was crystal clear.

And in that moment, I created a picture. My decision that I would be more loveable if I were truly thin was based on what I told myself in that moment of pain.

We also get pictures from our parents. With loving intention, they teach us everything they've decided about life and what's possible. Most of the time, those lessons are based on painful experiences from their own timelines. Their lessons may or may not fit for who we are.

Some pictures might even be from past life experiences. (Just skip over this idea if the concept of past lives isn't a fit for you.) Over the years of reading and healing others, I've seen many souls working to unravel decisions and limitations created in previous incarnations.

Each decision, or picture, has a message and a vibration. And, it will be reflected in one or more facets of life.

In the picture I shared earlier, the message was: "If I were thinner, I'd be more lovable." The vibration was pain. The picture was reflected in subsequent experiences in my relationships with men and in my relationship with my body.

When I eventually healed that pain and released the message, I created a new reality, and experienced a completely different reflection.

Inventorying Your Reality

Taking stock of the pictures through which you are manifesting reality is a key component to spiritual awareness and joyful living. The inventory is a journey. We can decide which to keep, change or discard.

Being willing to look at your decisions takes some spiritual gumption. Accepting that they are decisions and that they are changeable takes outright courage. You've got both. You are not your pictures. **You are a spiritual being on the journey of human experience, free to make a new decision and create a brand new day.**

As you become experientially aware that you can change decisions and get a new reality, your sense of yourself grows profoundly. Who is the you that can see the decisions as choices and change them? That's you as Spirit Self, a much vaster you than the part who lived them as truth.

The Human Self will often defend the photo album, the story, even when it's painful to hold on to. Changing reality invites you to see yourself beyond your perceived identity. Why not accept the call?

Consider your life for a moment. Is there an area that's just not flowing well? Your work, family relationships or the adventure of intimate partnership?

Notice if you're willing to realize what you've decided is true in this area. Are you sticking to your story or are you open to change?

Do you like the truths you've chosen? Changing a belief is the beginning of changing reality.

Now, I do realize that sounds good, but what about really doing it. It's one of those things that's simple, but not always easy. The picture or decision is the seed of reality. From the seed, we've grown entire experiences, histories and conditions in our lives. Those can be some big trees.

Notice that the tree has grown because of the seed. The decisions create experiences that reflect what's been decided. I know that it seems like the other way around. It feels like the experiences prove the decision, but think of the seed and the tree. With a different decision, you'll get a brand new tree.

This paradigm shift is crucial. With it, you become a powerful creator of your life. Without it, you remain the victim of your story. The leap is yours to take, and it will transform your life.

Changing the Picture

As we undecide a truth, we take our energy out of it. The experience itself is of value, even if it was painful. The experience itself cannot be destroyed. Extracting your energy from it and releasing decisions that affect reality are what matters. Then, the experience is transformed into wisdom instead of pain.

At the same time, we can entertain a new truth. We can plant a new seed and choose to tend the new growth with the amazing commodity of our attention.

Whatever we give attention to gets stronger. Some people are extremely famous simply based on the amount of attention they receive, will no actual achievements or contributions. They are a study in the power of attention.

Your attention is a resource, like time. But, most of us aren't mindful about how we spend attention.

Often we give more attention to what we don't want than what we would like. We can become more skillful with this resource, placing attention on what we'd like to make stronger.

We can choose to give the new truth more attention than the old. Here's a meditation process to do just that.

Meditation to Make a New Decision

First, start out by meditating. Walk through the steps outlined in Chapter 6 of Part 1. It's always important to be in your space and connected with your Spirit Self as you work with reality and your energy management tools.

Let Go of the Old
• Notice an old truth to release. You might distill it down to a statement. For example; "I'll never find a partner."
• Envision a container before you. You might choose a bubble, balloon, golden trash bag or rose.
• Imagine putting the old truth into a container. You could see it like a thought form coming out of your head and into the container. Allow it to come out of the chakras and aura too. Or, you could intend: Energy that says "insert old truth here" comes out of your body, your chakras and your aura and goes into the container.

• Sit and look at the old truth for a moment. Be willing to stop putting your energy into this decision.

• Consciously call your energy out of the old truth by creating a big gold sun above your head. Imagine your energy coming out of the old truth and into the gold sun.

• *Note:* You are NOT calling back the old truth. You're simply extracting energy you've given it and reclaiming your own energy back for yourself.

• Bring the gold sun into your body, filling yourself up with your own energy.

• Toss away the container with the old truth inside and destroy it.

Bring In the New

• Give your attention to the new truth by practicing believing it as you meditate. Imagine not only saying it, but experiencing it.

• You could even create a new gold sun above your head; put the new truth in a gold sun by seeing words go into it. Then, bring the sun in to your body.

• As you practice, if reasons come up that the new truth can't be so, simply release the reasons with a container.

• Replace them with a gold sun of an energy you'd rather have; perhaps freedom, joy, amusement or havingness.

You are reseeding your reality and rewiring your brain to create a new experience. That's your Human Self and Spirit Self in cooperative action!

As you practice and become more familiar with this process, you may actually see the moment of decision, the picture, in your imagination. If that happens, put the picture itself into the container, call your energy out of it and release it. This is called "blowing the picture."

In the time of transition between an old picture and the new, the old truth may put forth reasons to defend itself. Don't argue with an old truth or try to convince it of the new truth. Instead, simply let the old go and bring in the new.

As I mentioned earlier, taking stock of reality and creating anew is a journey. Please be gentle with yourself. You have created your reality without realizing you had the power to create differently. Be happy with yourself for even looking at this. You are a spiritual warrior.

LIVING SPIRITUAL AWARENESS

CHAPTER 4: NEUTRALITY AND RESISTANCE

Neutrality is having what is. Resistance is its counterpart. You can guess which is the more powerful stance of consciousness!

You've probably heard that what you resist persists. I'd take that a step further and say that what you resist controls you.

If you are bothered to distraction by the fact that something exists or is happening, that thing dominates you. It's got you; whether it's a person, a situation or anything at all.

For example, if you don't like how someone is behaving, and you aren't going to feel better until they change, they are in control of your reality. When you can allow that this is happening, when you can have it, you become free to choose your response from a place of inner power.

Resistance is non-havingness. The vibration of resistance may feel like anger, anxiety, fight, blame, judgment or reasons for wrongness.

Refusal to accept a prevailing reality creates a 'no' in our energy field and that leads to stuckness. Allowing or saying "yes, this is" creates a "yes." With yes, there's fluidity and broader possibilities for change.

Wisdom Hidden in the Conflict

Resistance isn't a complete waste of time. There's information in the struggle. When you find yourself in resistance, be willing to look at what's activated within you. Opportunities for finding old pain still at play today are everywhere. Resistance points to the pain. By listening to the fight, we can find and clear the old and outmoded.

As I write today, I'm in the process of selling a condo. I bought the place in 2004 and lived there for only a couple of years. I kept it as a rental and, because real estate went down with the big crash in 2009, I kept it longer than expected. Now, ten years later, it's on the market.

The selling process so far has been an up-and-down roller coaster of emotion. Twice, buyers have called after showings to say they love the place and plan to make an offer. Twice, they have disappeared.

Last night, I was upset with it all. I meditated. The reality is that this seems to be how selling a condo works these days. It isn't personal to me.

Often things feel so personal, and in one way they are. In one way, everything is personal because it plays out in our personal Universe. In another way, nothing is personal because, from the other person's view, it's about their Universe, not ours.

The disappearing buyers have no intention of hurting my feelings, they are just busy on the journey of house-hunting, and free to change their minds.

It's both always about you and never about you. Take a moment and consider that. It's amazing. With self-awareness and your spiritual skills, you have complete choice and control in how anything affects you.

If I resist the selling process, if I personalize it, then the people are unkind and the process is a problem. If I can allow that this is what the process of selling the condo looks like, I can come to neutrality. Allowing it without necessarily enjoying it, it doesn't control my space. If I resist, it's got me – my time, my energy, my precious attention.

When a particular person or situation riles you up, notice what you're saying to yourself in your inner reality.
- In what way is it personal?
- Is there someone else you are reminded of?
- Is something from the past illuminated?

Resistance is often a clue toward something within you that's up for healing.

Resistance is almost never a response to what's happening in present time. The gift of resistance is to show you where you're carrying an energy you don't need or a picture (a reality decision described in the previous chapter).

Finding the Picture

In my meditation on the real estate process, I noticed that some of my discontent was simply a healthy, human reaction to disappointment. I also became aware of a picture in my space: Me, my older sister and my brother sitting at a diner in New Jersey late at night. I'm eleven years old. My sister had taken us out of the house after I walked in on a particularly brutal fight between my parents.

I thought we were never going back. I was so happy. When I realized we'd be heading home, the disappointment was crushing. Of course, my sister, only seventeen at the time, couldn't take us anywhere else. But, my eleven-year-old self thought we were out.

The disappointment of the potential buyers saying one thing and then doing another illuminated that old picture for me. Both incidents involve a response to disappointment and expecting one thing but getting another.

I would have sworn I had healed that years ago, but another layer had surfaced. With gratitude, I took the opportunity to acknowledge the eleven year old within, clear old disappointments from my space and come more fully into present time.

Another example: When I train ministers for our non-denominational spiritual sanctuary, they often arrive to the program with an unpleasant history around religion. Early on, I ask them to sit in meditation and look at a rose for the word "church." They watch their energy for judgmental thoughts, past experiences and old beliefs. We clear them, coming to a space of neutrality with the word. When they can sit with that rose and be smooth, that's neutrality.

They can then come into the sanctuary in present time, without the burdens of the past clouding their actions and availability.

When we find ourselves emotionally activated in any way, that's an opening. Instead of wanting whatever has us stirred up to go away, we could explore. Is there a picture or belief in our reality that is illuminated by what's happening? The activation is a gift to inspire us to clear our own space.

Fighting what is takes a lot of energy. It's spiritually exhausting and demands large quantities of the commodity of our attention. Neutrality is so much lighter.

Here's a simple and effective meditation for beginning to come to neutrality with something you resist.

Meditation for Finding Neutrality

Before walking through the steps below, find your space by meditating. Follow the process outlined in Chapter 6 of Part 1 to ground and get your energy flowing. Connect with your Spirit Self by meditating before continuing on.

Run Neutral Energy
• Imagine a color that represents neutral Earth energy for you. That color may be unique to you and may change

daily. Just ask with your imagination, what color represents neutral Earth energy today?

• Once you notice the color, change your Earth energy to that hue.

• Do the same for your cosmic energy. Ask the questions and then adjust your cosmic energy accordingly.

• Now, you're running neutral.

Clean Out Resistance

• Next, clean out resistance.

• Create a rose to represent someone or something you resist. The rose is a symbol for their energy or for the situation.

• Sit in meditation in the presence of this rose and watch what happens in your inner landscape of thought and emotion. Be gentle and don't judge yourself.

• When resistance comes up (it may feel like anger, anxiety, fight, blame, judgment or reasons for wrongness), clear it.

• Imagining putting the thoughts, feelings or energies into a container (like a rose, bubble or balloon).

• When full, toss the container away and destroy it.

Fill Yourself In

• Fill yourself with gold suns of the vibration of neutrality, havingness, amusement, or a combination of these to replace what you're releasing.

Stick with this for a while, repeating the process of clearing. With highly charged situations, you might revisit this cleansing frequently. You'll be amazed at how your thinking changes as you clear.

Remember when we talked about the willingness to be uncomfortable as a spiritual skill? That comes into play here. In order to release resistance and come to neutrality, we get to give up being "right" and the other person or situation being "wrong." That can feel awkward at first.

It's not that you come to a place of enjoying this person or thing. It's that you don't need them or it to change in order to be ok in your own skin. From that empowered place, you will be much more creative in how you deal with this. Possibilities for change increase many-fold.

LIVING SPIRITUAL AWARENESS

CHAPTER 5: THE CRISIS FOR WOMEN

The crisis of spiritual amnesia is particularly poignant for women. Most of us live in a state of chronic self judgment and discontent.

Women are natural protectors and nurturers. We are also instinctive improvers and visionaries.

In the current culture, our very nature is turned against us. We aren't taught about our female abilities. No one guides us to manage the instinctive forces within. Absent needed wisdom and tender self-care, we become the affect of these drives rather than their master.

By connecting with our Spirit Self, we can turn this around. We can be gentler with ourselves and treat our natural drives, as well as our bodies, as the treasures they are.

When Nurturing Goes Wrong

The female body is genetically programmed to respond to the suffering of others.

We react to crying children and global injustices with fervor. Of course, men do too. But women are driven to answer pain with a particular urgency. It's a great strategy for the survival of the species.

This protective energy can get out of hand. For some women, it is nearly unbearable to be aware of the suffering of others. A combination of energetic sensitivity and the natural inclination to care create a drive to take on the problems of others.

We may find ourselves caretaking grown children, intimate partners, co-workers or friends to the degree that we are more responsible for their lives and challenges than they are. It feels like the right thing to do. But, it's really about "fixing" them so that we feel ok inside. That awful dread of someone suffering is calmed when we step in.

While living in Oregon, I went on a walk one unusually sunny morning. Along the way, I saw a kitten drowsing in the gutter. Yes, a kitten in the gutter. My protective instinct flared. I approached the kitten and it ran away, as if to say "no thanks."

But I couldn't hear. I was lost in an inner dialog that the kitten must be helpless and hungry. I went home, got a carrier and food, and "rescued" the kitten. I had actually trapped it. As soon as it was in the box, it began banging its head against the gate. Still, I couldn't hear. I called around and found a friend to take the animal.

While getting in the car, the kitten escaped. Now the little thing was miles from its home territory. I searched and searched to no avail. I began leaving food outside, which was eaten by something for a few days. But I never found the cat. My greatest hope is that the kitten found its way home.

I'm grateful for the lesson this baby illuminated. It was fine. It was feral. My actions were all based on the story I told myself about its imagined suffering and my female drive to heal. The kitten reminded me to leave some things alone.

When we over-nurture, we become an out-of-control healer, or OOCH. If you catch yourself doing this, notice if it's really about you feeling ok inside when you have helped the other person.

Check in. Maybe your nurturing is just what's needed for someone in trouble to take a step up. There are certainly times when helping is exactly the right thing to do.

However, if you're taking on too much, if your helping is really enabling, or if you're doing more to heal a person than they are; it's not a healthy use of your natural power.

In the end OOCHing hurts the healer, because we become responsible for what we can't control. And, by fixing things, we rob the other person of the problem they've created. They've produced the challenge in their journey of self-growth. When we take it away, they don't get their lesson and have to recreate a similar situation all over again.

This dynamic is out in the light and often discussed at psychological levels. Often we hear women say, "I just can't let go." Or, "I can't let my child live on the street" when referring to an addict adult. Mother's pain is understandable. If she had more mastery of her natural, body-based instincts, it might be easier to manage.

Do you find yourself helping out your partner, friends or grown children at your own expense? Are you an OOCH? Can you imagine being comfortable in your own skin while witnessing the sometimes painful journeys of others? It is possible.

Notice that it's natural to want to help. And, consider bringing some spiritual wisdom into the process. When we are in touch with ourselves as spiritual beings, we can use our natural care-taking to support others, but without becoming responsible for their lives.

Use your Meditation for Living tools before jumping in.

Ground, find your space, run your energy and consider: Are you really helping or are you interfering with someone's path of learning so you can relax and breathe? Will you feel better when they feel better? If so, step back. Wait, and live through your own discomfort, so you can witness and support their growth instead of sabotaging their lesson.

Not Good Enough?

Females are not only natural nurturers, we are also improvers. Do you notice that you never feel good enough? Or, perhaps something else isn't good enough; your job, your partner or your bank account? Are you always focused on changing your body or the next project on your house? For most women, the list never seems to end.

The drive to enhance is the result of a natural force within all female bodies called female creative energy (FCE). FCE is separate and apart from female energy and creative energy. Everyone, men and women alike, has creative energy. Both genders also carry both male and female energies, but only women have FCE.

Whenever I talk about female energy, male energy and FCE it's important to make some clarifications. I'm not talking about personalities, I'm talking about biological drive.

It's become dangerous to bring up the subject of unique female qualities because it highlights that men and women are different. The distinction can be perceived as an insult in light of our striving for equality in the world and workplace. We're getting there. But that's not what I'm talking about.

If we ignore our natures for social progress, we'll make the journey more effortful. By embracing what we are on a genetic level, we gain power.

Let's give ourselves permission to look at the biological energies unique to women and how to master them. If we pretend they aren't there, or that we're just like men, we become unconscious to a massive power within. And, we can be manipulated by it, instead of masterful over it.

In the Spirit Self, FCE sits in the aura in front of the second chakra. When a woman is pregnant, this energy flows into the second chakra and developing fetus, seeking out imperfections and correcting them. It's relentless in its pursuit and adjustment of anything less than exact precision.

This optimizing energy is crucial to the perpetuation of the species. It's a beautiful spiritual force.

When we're not pregnant, FCE will look for a place to run. It may run against your body, seeking out the perceived flaws and focusing on them with razor-like concentration. It may run against your partner; if only he or she would fix this or change that, everything would be ok.

In the current cultural paradigm, this blessed vibration is being used against us. Women are bombarded with messages and images of so-called "perfection." Who is deciding what's "perfect?" People selling products. They want you to buy their product and to buy into the illusion.

Most messages are cruelly directed at our bodies. Of course, the images are unattainable. They tap right into FCE and its natural pursuit of improvement. In comparison to the illusion, you'll never be good enough, and FCE vibrates in a chronic state of failure.

Only women will end this game, and it will happen when we recognize, treasure and master FCE. If you live in an ongoing state of body judgment, please stop that right now. It causes nothing but pain.

And, in the all-one consciousness, when you contribute self-hate toward the body, you add a drop to the massive energy that invites the next twelve-year-old girl into anorexia. Please, stop right now.

In advertising, most everyone looks like the "before" picture. That's why it's there – to grab you and your FCE and to tell you that you just aren't good enough. You could be better. What a scam.

It's simpler than you might think to step out of the game and begin to add to a future where women are truly empowered and free. When we ground FCE and calm it, everything begins to change.

The "to do" lists about our day, our bodies and our lives get much shorter. Things that seemed to matter so much don't feel important anymore.

Grounding FCE is a major step toward changing both the inner and outer worlds. I've outlined a meditation at the end of this chapter to help you get started.

A Side Note About Men

Sometimes men run a "not good enough" energy toward women. The process looks a lot like FCE in action, but it is entirely different.

Have you ever dated a man who criticized your body and your female emotions? If only you were thinner, more athletic and less emotional, it would all work out. In other words, if you were more like a man you would be good enough.

This male drive to "improve" a woman has to do with his fear and non-havingness for female energy, the beautiful female body and FCE. It's male control energy. There may have been hurtful dynamics between him and his mother. He picked up this fear somewhere along the line, but it's not your job to heal it. You can't. You've simply become the projection screen for his resistance.

If you encounter a man like this, I advise walking away. There are plenty of wonderful men out there who admire and celebrate real women. Go forth and allow one of those to treasure you as you deserve.

Women Love Potential

As if being natural protectors and improvers isn't enough, women are also born visionaries. If you consider the biology of the female body, it makes perfect sense.

Women take a single cell and create an entire human body. We seize possibility and build.

Women love potential; in a cell, in a house, in a man. We can see the promise of a future in a single seed. We can imagine a life-long marriage after just one date.

This tendency to envision becomes a problem only if we become emotionally invested in the imagined future as more than a possibility. It's perfectly fine to see potential and picture futures. Simply keep in mind that potential is only a possibility.

I worked with a client yesterday who is in the lovely beginnings of a relationship with a man. She's taken some classes with me and wanted to know how she could stop thinking about the future. I explained that she was asking herself not to be female and encouraged her to **come out of self-judgment and manage the energy instead of wanting it to go away.**

You're going to do it. Just remember to maintain perspective. When we become overly involved in an imagined timeline, our natural tendency to build will go into failure if the possibility doesn't unfold.

To calm emotional investment in potential, ground FCE and the ovaries. Even if you don't have physical ovaries in your body currently, if you were born a female, you have energetic ones. It sounds silly, but it's amazing. I've included the grounding of ovaries in the meditation below.

Before walking through the steps below, find your space by meditating. Follow the process outlined in Chapter 6 of Part 1 to ground and get your energy flowing. Connect with your Spirit Self by meditating before continuing on. It won't take long, and will make these next steps much more effective.

Meditation for the Female Body

Ground Female Creative Energy
• Become aware of the reservoir of Female Creative Energy (FCE) that sits in front of the second chakra energy center (chakras are explained in Chapter 4 of Part 1).
• Imagine the FCE sitting in a bubble in front of the second chakra. The bubble may be the size of a soccer ball or larger. Simply notice it, however is natural for you.
• There are two ways to ground the FCE bubble. You could extend a grounding cord from the bottom of the FCE bubble into your main grounding cord, like a branch on a tree. Or, you could extend a grounding cord from the bottom of the FCE bubble directly to the center of the Earth. Try it both ways and see which is right for you.

Dial It Down
• Imagine a dial on the bubble. Yes, a dial. Pretend the dial has settings; perhaps high, medium, low, and idle (or calm). Imagine turning your FCE dial to idle (or calm).
• Take a nice, deep breath and in a moment or two to let yourself notice the shift.

Ground the Ovaries
• Next, ground the ovaries by extending a small grounding cord from each ovary into the main grounding cord. Imagine unrealized potentials grounding out, freeing your creative force to build what's real in present time.
• If you'd like, pause for another good breath and a few moments to notice what's happening in your inner landscape of thought and emotion.

Come Home from the Future
• If you're emotionally invested in a potential future, imagine calling your energy back from that timeline with a big gold sun:
    o See a gold sun above your head.
    o Imagine calling your energy back from the unmanifested future.
    o Watch the gold sun get bigger as it fills with your energy.
    o Pop or drop the sun and fill yourself in, giving your life force back to yourself in present time.
• Note: it may feel like keeping your energy in the future will help it manifest. The opposite is true. **You can only create from present time.**

Be With Yourself

• Sit with your grounded female body for a time. Give yourself gold suns of self-love and appreciation, or any energies that feel right to you.

• If you'd like, practice appreciating your body with your thoughts. You could even imagine saying, "I love you body." Notice how this amazing statement is received by your physical self. Ground out any energies that argue with your body's beauty and value.

• Be wildly happy with yourself for taking back your power and beginning to treasure your beautiful female self.

I'd suggest practicing this meditation frequently, perhaps a couple of times a week. You'll notice a profound difference in how you feel about yourself and your life. You'll be calmer, have more clarity and a lightness about you that makes everything easier.

Another Suggestion

I would also submit this idea as a meditation for all women: use the Meditation for Living skills to clean out the energy from every sexual partner you've ever had. Additionally, call your energy back from each one.

Whenever women have sex, they give some of their energy to their partner. Men don't necessarily. They might, but with women it's a given.

LIVING SPIRITUAL AWARENESS

CHAPTER 6: CONTROL

As we journey the path of spiritual growth, recognizing the Spirit Self, we tend to see certain aspects of life with a refreshing perspective. Concepts like control, competition, family, money and relationships take on new meaning. We'll be looking at them all as we go forward. Let's explore control now. It's a spicy one!

As we get to know ourselves as spiritual beings through our Meditation for Living practice, we transition from seeking to control that which is around us to noticing we can only be in command of what is within. It's a lovely switch.

For purposes of discussion here, let's say when we try to force a change in something outside of ourselves, that's "false control." And, when we command our internal Universe of reality, that's "spiritual control."

Without self awareness, we can easily be compelled to exert false control in an attempt to force change when we want someone or something to be different than it is.

What's the Issue?

It may seem like the problem is our lazy partner, that bossy co-worker, the slow driver in the fast lane or whatever is going on. But what's really the challenge is our internal reaction, our response to whatever is before us.

Think about it for a moment. The "issue" is never the issue. What we tell ourselves about the person or circumstance will determine our well-being.

Sometimes when we push for change, the person or thing outside of us really does shift, and we feel better – for now. But we haven't grown. The button inside us that got pushed is still there. The next time a similar situation unfolds, we'll be right back where we started.

Even if we get what we want through false control, we are still giving our power away, because our internal peace is subject to something outside of us. That makes us a victim to whatever is happening.

What if all we needed to control was our own internal Universe of reality? Really, that's all we can control anyway. Kind of a relief, isn't it? And, it's so much easier than trying to control the world!

It's OK to Not Feel OK

This transition from false control to spiritual control requires us to accept sometimes feeling uncomfortable. We've discussed this notion just a couple of chapters ago in the section on Resistance and Neutrality. It's an important concept and deserves a revisit.

Allowing discomfort without having to take action to make the pain go away is a spiritual skill.

We can become comfortable with emotional discomfort by using our Meditation for Living skills and by keeping spiritual perspective in mind. We can't always see the bigger picture of what a person is up to, or why a particular situation is unfolding. When we can sit with it, and just let it be, we allow more possibilities of change and healing than if we jump in and try to fix it or change it.

Instead of exerting false control, we can use the situation as an inspiration to look within and notice the belief or fear that has us emotionally activated. Then, we can address that inner pain directly.

We can find the picture, or decision point, that generates the pain and clear it. Clearing a picture was discussed in Living Spiritual Awareness - Chapter 3: Decision Points. As we release decisions that don't work for us, we become free to respond to any situation with personal power and choice.

For example, a certain client comes to our student healing clinics and has become somewhat dependent on her monthly clearings. The clinic will soon be closing as we move to a new location, and this woman has been upset about the change. She's adamantly expressed her desire that we somehow keep the clinic going, and even had a few suggestions as to how that might work. She's hoping to control the situation, instead of looking at her disappointment and fear around the shift.

I've offered her several options to receive training to clear her own energy, all of which she's refused. She has given her power away to the student healers – she "needs" them. I'll continue to offer alternatives and support her as I invite her to look within.

I'm hoping she'll use the opportunity to clear herself of the belief that she can't change her own energy. Imagine how much more powerful she'll become, both with her spiritual skills and in the world in general, when she sees that she is just as capable as the healers she seeks.

Some Things Are Just Annoying

Maybe something is just simply aggravating. There's no picture to find, no growth to be had. Perhaps someone is just being rude or thoughtless. That's no reason to give up your inner contentment.

For instance, as I write, a neighborhood dog is barking. This dog barks often, loudly and for long periods of time. He's a greyhound who doesn't like to be alone. I've never met the owners, but I imagine they aren't equipped to meet the needs of this particular breed.

I have a choice. I can get upset. I can say to myself that the noise is so bad that I cannot think or write. Or, I can ground, release my irritation and continue to write while the dog barks. Sure, it's a little distraction, but the words keep coming.

This example shows that false control and resistance are closely linked. If I go into resistance, I won't be ok until the dog stops barking. I'll want to control what's out of my reach.

If I don't resist, if I vibrate at havingness for what is, I'm much freer to regulate my inner world instead. And, my internal experience is well within my realm.

A Reminder of the Third Chakra

When we try to force change, we are misusing the power of the third chakra. As you may remember from Part 1, the third involves our personal power, will and drive. It's the "action chakra" or do-er.

Ideally, the action of the third chakra brings the vision of the seventh chakra (spiritual truth) at the top of the head into physical manifestation. When someone is disconnected from their seventh, the third chakra often tries to take over.

At the end of this chapter I've included a meditation for calming the third chakra and empowering the seventh.

True Control

Ultimately, we can't control anything but our own space. Someone may allow us to control them, but that is by their agreement. They are in charge and can change the agreement at any time.

We can control our energy and our choice of response to what happens around us. There are times in life when an appropriate response is grief, sorrow, anger or pain. But in most situations, we have a choice of a range of responses to a situation.

Should you lose a job, you'll decide whether this is a tragedy or a temporary challenge leading to new opportunity. Your decision will affect your well-being, your physical health and your stance of consciousness in the world.

Your energetic viewpoint will affect the range of possibilities of reality. Resistance to what is narrows the possibilities, just like a funnel. The more fear, the tighter the funnel. An open stance allows a wider range.

Spiritual control is different than repression. It would be unhealthy to use spiritual control to avoid feeling how we feel. That would just be using our skills to stuff unpleasant feelings down into the chakras, where they would fester and grow.

We must honor emotions but not let them rule our realities. If there's pain, feel it. Then choose. That's spiritual freedom in action; the freedom to command your space, to choose a reality.

Meditation for Controllers

Before walking through the steps below, find your space by meditating. Follow the process outlined in Chapter 6 of Part 1 to ground and get your energy flowing. Connect with your Spirit Self by meditating before continuing on.

First, Just Look
• Create a rose to represent the situation or person you feel a need to control. The rose is a symbol for their energy or for the situation.
• Sit in meditation in the presence of this rose and watch what happens in your inner landscape of thought and emotion.
• Notice what you fear and be with the discomfort. Be gentle and don't judge yourself.

Release Fear and Replace
- Release the fear by creating a container for it, a balloon, bubble or rose, and release it.
- Give yourself some gold suns to replace the fear, perhaps of the vibration of trust or self-love.

Shift the Concept of Control
- Create a rose outside your third chakra, in front of your body.
- Imagine the concept of control being removed from the third and moving into the rose.
- Bring the rose up to the top of your head, to crown chakra level.
- Approach the spinning seventh (or crown) chakra with the rose. Allow the pull of the chakra to grab the rose and draw it into the crown to be integrated there.
- Refill the third chakra directly with a big gold sun of permission.

Practice
- Notice an energy you'd like to be prevalent in your reality; perhaps joy, calm or peace.
- Imagine a rose near the crown chakra to represent the energy you've chosen. Alternatively, you could imagine a color to represent the vibration.
- Simply intend that the crown match the rose or the color.
- Notice the crown chakra shifting to the vibration you've chosen. This is an experiential event, there's no "how to" here. Just notice.
    - If other energies come up to argue, simply release them into containers.

• Intend that the body follows or matches the crown. Let the crown chakra drive the bus, or set the reality.

• Notice that you feel different. Your body is responding to the prevailing vibration, chosen by you.

Now, you're really in control!

LIVING SPIRITUAL AWARENESS

CHAPTER 7: COMPETITION

Let's explore the energy of competition next. There's the fun, healthy kind that happens in sports and games (when they aren't played with too much personal attachment). And, there's the destructive kind that happens when we compare ourselves to others. That's the flavor I'll be addressing here. When we practice this toxic competition, we rank or judge ourselves (or the other person) based on the perceived results of a comparative assessment.

Toxic competition and playful competition are completely different vibrations. In toxic competition, evaluation pits people or events against one another with a judgmental edge. And someone always comes up short. Someone or something is intrinsically better than the other. Judgment follows, usually of the self-deprecating variety.

Don't mistake inspiration for toxic competition. Studying someone to be inspired to create in a similar fashion is healthy. Perhaps you appreciate their ingenuity and want to bring forth your own brand of the same energy from yourself. You may admire them, but you are no less special and valuable as a person than they are.

Toxic competition is the opposite of unconditional acceptance. It invalidates the individuality of each spirit and each human. The reality that each being, each person comes to the moment with a different set of energies, experiences, pictures and karmic challenges is ignored in the contest.

When we're in competition, we've forgotten that each of us is a unique, individuated expression of the consciousness that creates this Universe. We've fallen into spiritual amnesia.

And the comparison doesn't happen through clear eyes. We make decisions about what the other person must be like according to our own histories and sense of ourselves. We see the other, and ourselves, through a fog of assumption.

My Friend Joan

I have a friend I'll call Joan. Joan exemplifies one of the current cultural definitions of beauty; super slim, long blonde hair, amazing blue eyes and a bright white smile. It's fun to go to lunch with her and watch the waiter swoon. It's not so fun to notice how people (mostly other women) assume she must be happy, wealthy and have it all, simply based on the way she looks.

I watch women go into competition with her on a body level and create a whole set of suppositions about her life. Compared to the picture of glamorous Joan, they almost always come up short. They respond by either putting her on a pedestal with envy or resisting her as they really resist the self-judgment she stirs within them.

In the process, they miss getting to know Joan. Of course, Joan has challenges and issues in her life. Wonderfully, she is neutral to the competition she encounters. Joan is a healer by profession and aware of this dynamic. She meets it with open-hearted compassion.

Win or Lose, You Lose

As Joan experiences, women practice toxic competition frequently on a body level, and are encouraged to do so by the current marketing culture and media presentation of females. This is one of the greatest tragedies of our time. What a waste of the precious resources of time, attention and energy, not to mention female wisdom.

Acknowledging and being aware of this type of competition is a great step. Still, sometimes you may get stuck in it. If you are in a female body this lifetime, notice if you judge yourself in response to other women. If you notice you're thinner, heavier, prettier or not; and the outcome affects how you feel about yourself or her, you're caught!

A quick wake-up call is to remember the perspective of the newly dead. No one has ever returned from a near-death experience to report that their body was fat and ugly when they viewed it from above. Instead, they attempt to convey an indescribable beauty and grace.

Competition can go both ways – sometimes we seem less than and sometimes we seem more than another in some area. Either way, we lose. We've lost our awareness of uniqueness. Just as damaging, our inner peace has become subject to the condition of another person or thing outside of us.

Rays of the Same Sun

We're each a unique and magnificent part of the consciousness that creates this Universe. We're rays of the same sun, each ray expressing particular facets of the all-one. Competition between rays just doesn't make sense.

When we know ourselves to be a part of the whole, not just intellectually but experientially, we can celebrate the differences. We acquire that wisdom through continued practice of the Meditation for Living skills, remaining mindful that we, and everyone else, are spiritual beings on the human journey; and by being in touch with our Spirit Self, our energy.

For example, in my reading practice, I'm really good at uncovering unseen influences and clearing them. And, I'm exceptional (if I do say so myself) at uncovering belief systems that generate reality and disrupting them, creating space for a new experience. I see the journey and intentions of the soul before me and clear the path for that soul to create through the personality identity. On occasion, I see a spirit who has passed and receive messages from them.

I have a colleague, Linn, who is great at communicating with the dead, and speaks with deceased relatives in almost every session. She's spectacular at receiving their messages and conveying the communication with great detail.

We're different. Both styles have value and a place in the world. I don't need to see more dead people to be a better reader and she doesn't need to do deeper healing work to be more effective. We can both just be who we are, and let it shine.

When we are awake and aware of both our uniqueness and our belonging, we can find our distinct talents and express them freely. And, we can support others in doing the same without secretly enjoying it should they fall. Have you noticed the satisfaction some folks experience when someone who has been popular and successful falls from grace? That pleasure is just a reflection of inner pain.

Now, just because you resign from the competition game, that certainly doesn't mean others will follow suit. Most folks get caught up in toxic competition on a daily basis. If you find yourself in a situation where someone is in competition with you in this personal way, it's helpful to simply acknowledge what is happening without participating.

Acknowledging and simply having the moment is different than surrender. Conceding is a form of engaging in the competition game. Instead, ground and use your basic tools. You can also engage a technique called "body of glass."

Body of Glass

Body of glass is a fun and effective practice to use when energy is coming at you. You do need to be grounded to use it, but at this point you can do that in a short moment, right? See the cord and, boom, you're grounded.

To be at body of glass, imagine being transparent just like a clear window or goblet. Not fragile like glass, it's the see-through quality we're looking for here. **Imagine that anything coming towards you moves right through you.**

This is a great emergency technique. You might use it when you notice competition, anger or any unpleasant energy in the air or directed your way. When used along with protection roses, you are very unlikely to pick up any negative energy.

You probably won't be able to hold it for long, and you don't need to. Body of glass is a place to go for a moment or two, you wouldn't want to live there.

You vs. You

Even our relationship with ourselves can easily become mired in compare/compete energy. Do you find that where you are isn't good enough compared to where you believe you should be? Of course, it's healthy and productive to have goals and move toward them. But if we aren't enough as a person until we get there, that's competition.

It happens. We create a picture of where we think we should be and imagine we'll be good enough when that condition manifests. Perhaps when we reach a certain number on the scale, we'll love our body. Or, be at peace when a there's a certain number in the checkbook. The desired condition is called a "perfect picture."

A perfect picture says: "When this thing is perfect, I'll be ok." It's easy to go into competition with the picture and come up short in present time. And, even if the "perfect" condition does manifest, the self-judgment that created it will persist, often moving to another topic.

What if you are worthy, wonderful and completely lovable right now? Then, the goal or change is an expression of self-love and being good to yourself. When you create from self-love; the vibration, journey and outcome are set at that energy. When you create through competition and punishment energy (not good enough), the journey and outcome are set right there.

Body vs. Spirit

Yet another way competition can play out is in the relationship between body and spirit. Think of people who give their power away to a spirit guide or being, just because that entity is not incarnated. The theory is that, by virtue of being non-physical, the entity must be smarter or know the future. The undercurrent energy suggests that being without a body is better than having one.

But incarnation is the highest adventure of the soul. **It's a brave and wonderful undertaking to join in the Earth school.** Energy that would suggest otherwise is similar to religious dogma, with the whole original sin thing, the desires of the flesh being wrong and all that mythology.

Enjoy Being You

As a spiritual being, you are eternal. You exist and continue outside time. Incarnation is the opposite. Each lifetime is singular and will never repeat. There's only one time of me being Lauren Skye. The soul that is me will re-manifest in a new form, a new personality, a new life.

There's only one time of you being you. Instead of comparing yourself to others, perhaps you will choose to enjoy being you, the one and only you.

Meditation for Competitors

Before walking through the steps below, find your space by meditating. Follow the process outlined in Chapter 6 of Part 1 to ground and get your energy flowing. Connect with your Spirit Self by meditating before continuing on.

First, Just Look
• Become aware of someone with whom you are in competition. Create a rose to represent their energy or simply see their picture before you.
• Sit in meditation in the presence of this rose or picture.

Consider Some Questions and Sit with Them
• Notice: What's not good enough about you in the comparison?
• What are you not seeing about yourself by being in that game?
• What's not good enough about the other person?
• What are you not seeing about the other person?
• Simply let yourself sit, run your energy and notice what comes up in your awareness.
• Be gentle and don't judge yourself. Instead, be happy with you for looking at these dynamics and empowering yourself.

Release Competition and Replace
• As you sit with the rose or picture, release competition.
• Create a rose, bubble or balloon and imagine releasing competition energy from your space. You may notice it come from particular chakras, and that these may correspond to the topics where competition plays out in the relationship.

- Let the container fill, release it and destroy it. Repeat as many times as you'd like.
- Replace the competition energy with gold suns of whatever you'd rather have.
- Suggested vibrations would be freedom, clarity, amusement, havingness and self-love.

Step It Up With Gratitude
- If you are moved to do so, you might imagine being grateful to this person for inspiring you to learn more about yourself.

Let Go and Fill In
- Release the person's energy and call your own back to you.
- If you are looking at a picture, put the picture in a rose. If you are looking at a rose, skip this step.
- Allow any of this person's energy you are carrying to go into the rose.
- Toss the rose far away and destroy it, freeing their energy.
- Create a gold sun above your head. Intentionally call your energy back from the person into the sun, watch it get big, fill yourself in and receive your energy back.

Enjoy a brand new level of awareness and freedom!

LIVING SPIRITUAL AWARENESS

CHAPTER 8: FAMILIES AND AGREEMENTS

As I write this morning, my mother lays in a hospice facility, hours or perhaps minutes from making her transition back to spirit. She has had no food or water for four days and is no longer able to speak. That she's still alive is a testament to how amazing the body is.

As Spirit Self, she's in and out of her body, gathering information. Packing up, and getting ready for the next step of the adventure.

Our journey together has been an intense one. Instead of healing her profound pain from childhood abuse, she stuffed it with whiskey and food. I'm the youngest of six, and for many years it was just her and I and her pain in the house. My father was there, but not present.

As the alcoholism progressed, so did the rage. Suffice it to say ours was not a happy household.

I dove into the healing journey as an adult. Mom wouldn't talk about the past or even the possibility of spiritual reality. Our conversations became more and more heated. We spent some years in separation after a more-than-tense visit at her seventieth birthday celebration. After about seven or eight years with no communication, I began waking up in the middle of the night.

In the dark I heard her voice, saying, "Call me, call me, call me." At first I resisted. With defiance, I'd reply in thought, "No, you call me."

These pre-dawn "visits" went on for a couple of weeks and eventually became exhausting. So, I wrote her a letter to say hello and see if she'd like to reconnect. She called me right away and said, "I was so glad to get your letter because I've been sitting in my living room every night thinking 'call me, call me, call me'."

I explained that those messages are delivered at about 2:00 am, so please use the phone from now on! When we did talk, it was uncomfortable for a few minutes, but that passed quickly as the walls came down on both sides.

"I'm ready for what you do," she said.

I was thrilled! And, we both tried. But Mom quickly hit block after block in the process. She would say it was just too painful to face, and I would remind myself that, in my reality, there is nothing too painful to heal.

I gave readings, I sent class recordings, I explained and explained. Still, she wouldn't have it. She continued to choose pain. I learned to respect her "no." Her chronic sorrow inspired me to leave no stone unturned in my own journey. So thank you, Mom, I am deeply grateful.

Everybody's Got One

Families; everybody's got one. If you've got a loving, supportive one, good for you. If you've got one that drives you crazy, good for you! And, if you've got one that's deeply wounded, good for you, too. No matter what the dynamics, families provide profound opportunities for spiritual growth and self-awareness.

These relationships largely define us on an ego-personality level. If needed, it's up to us to redefine. It's not what happened, it's what you do with what happened that matters.

What's really going on in a family group? A bunch of souls get together and make an agreement to come through into Earth. In spirit, everyone is excited about the lessons we'll clear, judgment we'll release and vibrations we'll explore. Maybe it's just me, but I imagine also being excited about physical sensations, like taste. I am grateful to be here in the time of pizza and French fries.

We make an agreement with our parents for a human body. Then, it gets physical. The pain we are so determined to clear as soul is activated and surfaces. The drama begins to unfold.

Because of the spiritual contracts, the intimacy of the physical proximity and the DNA bond, family relationships are our most highly charged. Believe it or not, in spirit we picked them.

When that choice is in the light, we can look at the dynamics through clearer eyes.

It's not that the timeline is planned in detail in advance. There are just general intentions. Perhaps, "I'll learn to love myself fully." Or, "I'll forgive myself for this or that past life mistake I'm holding against myself." Or, "we've been stuck together in a series of lifetimes, let's get unstuck this time...."

Like a trailhead with several forks all leading to the same peak, we choose the route.

There's no right or wrong. I know it really, really, really seems like there's right and wrong. There is in Earth, but not in spirit. To the journeying soul, every experience is of value. **We learn and mature not only as people, but as souls, through experience.**

May it be that we evolve to a place where pain is no longer. But for now, so it is.

I once watched an amazing video of Ramtha, a spiritual entity that is channeled by JZ Knight. During the talk, Ramtha shared a controversial concept. It may strike you as offensive at first, but bear with me. Ramtha said that the only way to know the 10 commandments are good ideas is to have broken them all. He added; otherwise you're just a righteous preacher.

Souls Journey and Gather

Think about that within the framework of reincarnation. As the soul journeys, we collect experiences. Experiences that aren't judged, translate into wisdom. Judgment is so powerful that it turns that which could be wisdom into karma. Releasing judgment is crucial.

Wisdom is wealth in spirit. The more well-travelled the soul along the range of experience, the more wise and the more autonomous to choose a reality.

The only way to understand why stealing isn't a great idea is to have been the one doing the taking and the one having the loss. Then, we get it.

The Duality of Earth and Spirit

Just because every experience is of value in spirit, that doesn't make it acceptable on Earth. This is a dichotomy that just can't be resolved, so please don't even try. Yes, on some level, being abused is of value to the spiritual soul gathering experience. And, NO, it's not ok on Earth. It's never ok. The two realities can't be reconciled.

Yet this is how it is. I trust there is greater purpose in everything; more than I can possibly perceive from this vantage point. As you explore reality for yourself, trust what you see as your truth.

Framing Pictures

Everything is how we frame it. Remember the earlier chapter on decision points, or pictures? The picture is what happens. What matters most is what we tell ourselves about it, what we decide. The frame we put around an event defines it, and us.

I could have decided that my mother taught me that life is just a series of painful experiences and betrayals. I've chosen instead to be inspired into spiritual awareness.

As I look around my family, it's interesting to notice how each of my siblings has framed the past in their own ways. How they've responded with their life choices, parenting styles and relationships with themselves along a diverse spectrum from anger to joy. It's a wonderful illustration of the power to choose.

I have a client, "Terry," who is actively working on reframing a childhood of maternal rejection and abuse. She's moving from angry victim to empowered woman. Using a combination of spiritual work and therapeutic support, she's revisiting her timeline and changing the decisions she's made about herself and the world along the way.

In a recent meditation on forgiveness, Terry clearly wasn't on board. I love that she can be right where she is. To rush or pretend wouldn't be real. In spirit, there is no hurry.

All by Agreement

Looking at families gives us the opportunity to consider the idea of spiritual agreement. Every family, every group, every couple, every friendship comes together by agreement.

An agreement is a spirit-to-spirit contract to do something, heal something, activate something or play a role for someone. An agreement can involve any sort of interaction or experience.

Some contracts are created before we come into incarnation, some are created during the course of a lifetime and some are carried forward from past lives.

As I've mentioned before, I'm on board with the concept of reincarnation. If you aren't, simply frame the information in the way that works for you. Even if we don't agree on the cyclical nature of life, we can look at agreements together.

Some agreements last just a moment or two, some a lifetime or more, and all possibilities in between. They're unfolding all the time.

We make an agreement with our parents for a body. We make agreements with our children, even pets. Women without children have interesting agreements with their pets (me included).

Supporting Cast

Some people agree to be supporting cast members in our lives. I cherish my agreement with my husband. He's loving, loyal and understands my commitment to my work.

Equally precious is my agreement with my stepdaughter, a beautiful spirit who welcomed me into her life at age fourteen. And my friend and colleague, Margaret, who always sees my capability and strength when I can't seem to find it.

Consider your life. Who's got your back? Notice those loving, nurturing agreements. And notice who you support too. These agreements add to the joy of living.

More Interesting Characters

Sometimes the roles people play in our lives get more exciting.

A student in class, "Barb," recently lamented her discomfort with an acquaintance, "Kim." Kim touches Barb with unwelcome hugs and shoulder massages and Barb doesn't like it. Yet, she says nothing. In fact, Barb often says nothing in situations she doesn't enjoy.

I can just see them as souls; Barb saying, "I'm going to learn to speak up for myself this time," and Kim saying, "Oh, I'll help you do that."

As a soul, Kim is giving Barb the opportunity to take a step. That's an agreement.

Here's another example: Many years ago I was in a coffee shop getting drinks for a TV crew before doing some community access broadcasting. I had eight orders to fill. A woman came up behind me in line and was clearly agitated, huffing with her breath and exuding an air of hurried overwhelm. I decided I would offer to let her step ahead of me.

I turned and said, "I'm going to be ordering eight coffees," but before I could finish my sentence, she screamed; "What? You don't want a black woman standing behind you?!" She was African-American, as were many of the customers and workers in the store. Denver isn't a segregated city.

I was shocked. This was clearly an energetic assault, not only a verbal confrontation. And, I admit, I lost my willing spirit. I simply said, "Wow" (a wonderful, simple response I learned from my friend Heidi). I turned my back, listened to her muttering about my being a white "B," and planned to slowly order all eight coffees. Within a few moments, she left the line and stormed off.

I heard hearty laughter from off in the corner. It was coming from the security guard. He gave me a wink and a knowing that this sort of thing had happened before. The barista communicated the same energy without saying a word – just with a smile and nod. Grateful for the support, I held my head high and breathed through the moment.

I closed my eyes, grounded and found my space (yes, right there and then) and looked at what was happening. First, I forgave myself for not offering her my spot. Then, I got clear.

The woman was seeing me through a picture, and she had anger to vent. By agreement, she chose me, a healer, who wouldn't match her rage. On some level, I contracted to be a part of the game. Perhaps I stepped in so that she didn't choose someone who would have enjoyed the fight. That's an agreement.

Why Make Agreements?

We make agreements to learn and experience. We might be motivated to take a step in growth, spiritual evolution or healing. We might be driven by a picture that controls us or by a deep belief that has us repeating a pattern. Maybe we're just giving a moment of healing.

Beautifully, agreements can change, begin and end. Like the future, agreements are fluid and malleable.

It takes two or more to create an agreement, but only one to change or end it.

Right now you may be thinking, "Great! How can I get that person who has agreed to be a pain in my neck out of my life right now?" If so, consider that agreements often illuminate pictures. That's a sort of healing contract, although it may not feel like it at the time.

Instead of wishing that person away, you might reflect in your meditations about the agreement. Consider:
• What are you learning?
• What are you teaching?
• What are you giving and receiving?
• Do you notice a picture, or belief, that surfaces when this person is around you? What does that remind you of from the past?

I've included a meditation on agreements at the end of this chapter with all of these questions and more.

When We Change

The meditation I've chosen includes a process for changing an agreement. Please know that, should you change an agreement, the other person may or may not agree to the shift. They may not be done learning from the situation. Or, they may not be finished experiencing pain on some level.

They may end the agreement in response to your change in order to create a brand new one with someone else to keep the learning (or pain) going. They have a divine right to do so.

I married my first husband at age twenty-six. I wasn't whole, and neither was he. We were two wounded people coming together.

Along the way, I found myself, my spiritual abilities and my path. I was the one who changed, and changed completely. We would joke that we would walk into a room but enter two different places; my seeing the situation one way and him seeing through a totally different reality. He is an atheist.

He chose to end our agreement. I'm grateful he did. It freed me to be more of myself and to bring in a partner who is in affinity with who I am in present time.

In one conversation over old credit cards, my ex said, "If I never hear the word energy again, it will be too soon." I smiled widely. Of course this is how he would feel!

Our marriage was over, so it was good to end the covenant. Really, when a contract is complete spirit-to-spirit, nothing can hold it together. When it's not done, nothing can tear it apart.

As you grow in spiritual awareness, your relationship with yourself grows. As that happens, agreements may shift. Amusement and havingness are good vibrations to remember in times of change. They were presented in Living Spiritual Awareness – Chapter One: The Transition.

Also, trust that if someone should turn away, you are not alone, ever. You as Spirit Self will call your next agreements to you in divine timing.

Meditation on Agreements

Before walking through the steps below, find your space by meditating. Follow the process outlined in Chapter 6 of Part 1 to ground and get your energy flowing. Connect with your Spirit Self by meditating before continuing on.

First, Just Look
• Become aware of an agreement you'd like to look at or shift.
• Create a rose to represent the agreement. The rose symbolizes all the energies contributing to your experience of this contract.

Find Neutrality
• Come to some neutrality by changing your Earth and cosmic energies to neutral colors (this technique is presented in LSA 4 Resistance and Neutrality).

Consider Some Questions and Sit with Them
• Stay in the center of your head (sixth chakra) as you consider some questions. If you fall into the emotional center (second chakra), simply find your way back to neutrality and the center of your head.
　　○ It's not that the emotions are wrong, it is just that there is a broader spectrum of information and possibilities when you're in neutrality in the sixth.
• What am I learning in this experience?
• What am I teaching in this experience?
• What am I giving in this experience?
• What am I receiving?
• What does this remind me of?
• What is the opportunity for growth?

Go Deeper?

• If you'd like to go deeper, see an imaginary contract next to the rose. Pretend to change the language regarding your part of the interaction. You don't have to see the exact words, like reading a piece of paper. Let it play out easily with your ability to imagine, without effort.

Change It or End It?

• If you change the agreement, imagine rolling up the altered contract and putting it in the rose. Toss the rose over your shoulder.

   o Watch what happens with your imagination. It will be caught by your spirit helpers.

• If you'd like to end the agreement, do this same exercise but imagine signing the agreement as completed. It is best to do this with a vibration of success and gratitude for what's been.

• If you're ending the agreement, the next step is the same. Imagine rolling up the closed contract and putting it in the rose. Toss the rose over your shoulder. It will be caught by your guides.

• Imagine releasing any energy from this person that you're carrying into a container (a rose, balloon or bubble) and let it go by tossing the container away and destroying it, freeing the energy.

Call Your Energy Home

• Call your energy back from the person with a big gold sun and fill yourself in, receiving that energy back for you.

PART 3: WALKING IN TWO WORLDS

INTRODUCTION: GOODBYE MOM

In the last chapter, I mentioned my mother was in hospice and nearing death. Now, she's left her body and passed fully to the spiritual plane.

Her life was a brilliant example of the fact that the energies we carry and the beliefs we hold shape our experience of life.

Molested as an adolescent, my mother, Sylvia, spoke up to her mother. My grandmother ignored the problem and the assaults continued. This, along with other myriad inappropriate family dynamics, led to a life based in unhealed pain.

Sylvia believed she wasn't good enough, that it wasn't safe to speak the truth and that she couldn't fulfill her dreams. All of these beliefs became her reality.

My mother gave up a moderately successful career as an actress early on and married a man with obsessive-compulsive disorder long before that disease was recognized. Back then, he was just seen as ridiculously controlling. I remember him oftentimes ignoring me as he engaged in tapping and counting rituals. This was Sylvia's life partner.

Mom birthed nine children. Three didn't make it. I am the youngest of six siblings. She used to joke that she liked her babies until they started to talk, a reflection of her own wounded voice within.

Over the years, society changed and help was available to address the past. Sylvia was too afraid to face the pain and instead chose to hold it. She lived in a victim stance of consciousness; overwhelmed, afraid and erratic. In the meantime, frustration and resentment stewed. She became a heavy drinker, and an angry one.

As I mentioned in the last chapter, Mom and I did eventually find a way to communicate, let love flow and allow each other be who we are, or were. When she was eighty years old, she let me give her an energy healing for the first and only time. As I worked, she squirmed and tensed. I realized just how uncomfortable she was in her own skin.

I've been watching my mother since her passing. On one level, yes, she's gone. On another, she's simply changed form, as we all will.

On the human plane, I'm grieving the loss of what was and what wasn't. I honor her life of sorrow, and I admit I do have some judgment. I wish it had been different. I remind myself that I can't possibly know the bigger spiritual picture unfolding for her as a soul.

Bridging to the spiritual level of reality, I've been watching and offering support as Sylvia looks back on what is now her most recent past life. For days I've been receiving images from the past, sent by Mom, with captions of explanation and apology.

She is waking up. She's seeing how her long-held pain, deep hurt and pent-up rage created her experience.

Hopefully, she's forgiving herself, releasing judgment and transmuting that pain to wisdom. If she doesn't forgive, that which she holds against herself will seed her experience of the next incarnation, with karma carried forward. Through the release of judgment, wisdom replaces karmic potentials.

We've talked briefly about "the perspective of the newly dead" before, in that people tend to appreciate their bodies in a new way when seeing them from the other side.

For most people, all of life is seen with brand new eyes when we step outside of it. This is a result of releasing spiritual amnesia. It's as though upon death we awaken, the fog clears and we can see the love, the light and the freedom to heal that was there all along.

We don't have to wait until death for freedom. When we are awake, we walk in two worlds. We can see life through a broad vision encompassing the beauty of both sides.

As for my mother, she lived her days deep in the fog of forgetfulness. What about you? You're still here. You have a choice.

As you've moved through this book, you've established a connection between your Human Self and Spirit Self. Your identity is becoming more and more founded in knowing yourself as a spiritual being.

You are awake, and, with your Meditation for Living skills, equipped to stay conscious and deal with what you see. You are becoming more and more free to have your human adventure with a spiritual perspective; to walk in two worlds.

WALKING IN TWO WORLDS

CHAPTER 1: THE BODY

In the next four chapters, I'll be sharing about what I like to call the "Big Four:" Health, money, work and relationships. These are the most commonly addressed areas in private reading sessions.

When we're awake, walking in two worlds, these concepts dramatically transform. What were once areas of stress and concern become recognized as beautiful expressions of energy and reflections of the inner landscape.

Let's start with health and the body because, without a body, the other concepts become a moot point. Yet, we take it for granted.

What's a Body?

I love this quote by Emmanuel, a beautiful spiritual being who was channeled for years by the late Pat Rodegast:

"The purpose of life is exploration.
Adventure. Learning. Pleasure.
And another step towards home.

Physical bodies
Are rather like space suits.

Your physical bodies can be symbols of restriction,
Of ultimate pain and death,
Of surprising and alarming needs
And of unexpected triviality
That knows no bounds of denigration.
Or they can be seen as chosen vehicles
That souls are inhabiting
Because, rather like space suits,
They are necessary where you are.

It is within your humanity
That you will learn
To recognize your divinity.

The spiritual and the human have to walk hand in hand
Otherwise the spiritual has no foundation
On which to take hold."

The Emmanuel writings are spectacular and I highly recommend them all. Check out Emmanuel's Book III: What is an Angel Doing Here? and go from there.

A Space Suit and So Much More

Your body is your space suit, your vehicle for navigating physical reality. It's also a sensory device and communication mechanism.

The body is always doing a perfect job of sensing the energy running through it and expressing those vibrations. Some energies feel good and others don't. The body expresses its reality physically, emotionally and mentally. We may experience the energies carried as sensation, feeling or thought.

The common premise is that the body responds to thought. But what creates the thought? Energy. Energy or vibration is the precursor to thought. Acknowledging the role of energy as the seed of thought is an important step in opening to the vastness of spiritual consciousness.

In creating change, you can think a new thought and begin to uncover the energy under the thought. The new thought will counter the old energy and bring it to light. Then, you can clear the old vibration. Practicing affirmations is a good example of this process.

But if you'll shift the energy first, it's much easier to hold the new thought. Once energy has shifted, the new thought will hold more naturally and require much less discipline or effort to embrace.

I have a friend who is a psychotherapist and we've debated this point. She believes thought creates energy. I believe energy is at the root of all, including thought. Look for yourself. Either way you see it; you can work with the body in a kind and graceful way.

Let's work with my theory for now.

The Right Gas for Your Car

As a general rule, the body runs best on your energy, the vibration resulting from your occupying the body as a spiritual entity.

Foreign energy is like the wrong gas for your car; it may run, but it will sputter, and likely be damaged in the long run.

When the body is expressing a painful energy, we often want to make it wrong. But that's just blaming the messenger, so to speak.

Perhaps you have digestive trouble and, of course, want it to go away. That's a reasonable desire. At the same time, it's helpful to notice what the body pain is representing; perhaps you're overstressed, exhausted or using food to handle emotional challenges.

Maybe your body is trying to tell you something. It's easy to make the body itself the problem. Instead, imagine listening to its constant flow of communication.

When we're attentive to the body's messages, we can use it's feedback to heal ourselves, even of old emotional pain, if we are willing.

The body responds to whatever energies are most prominent. You as spirit decide the energy. When we forget we are spirit, it feels like we can't choose. It seems like what's going on around us determines how we must feel.

When we say 'yes' instead of resisting whatever the body is expressing, we can use our Meditation for Living skills to change the energy that the body is reflecting, and so shift our condition. We can listen to what is happening instead of needing it to stop as soon as possible.

Meditate to become aware of the energetic root of an illness or pain:

- Find your space (walk through the steps outlined in Chapter 6 of Part 1).
- Imagine saying hello to your body and notice what happens.
- Allow whatever happens on an emotional or physical sensation level. This brings you into communication with your body.
- Ground the area of pain directly, releasing foreign energy. Bring in a gold sun of love and watch that spot fill up.
- Look at a rose to represent the symptom.
- Sit with it as you run your energy and notice what comes in your thoughts and feelings.

This energy has been stuffed into the body, so it may take a few sessions to find clarity. That's ok.

Sometimes it's genuine, authentic and appropriate to feel sorrow, anger or pain. But most of the time we have a range of choice in responding to something and a range of options in the energies we run through the body.

When we stop resisting our own body, our relationship with our physical vessel begins to transform.

In Sickness and In Health

Sometimes you just get sick and there's no meaning behind it. **Just because you keep your energy clear doesn't mean you'll never catch another cold.**

There's nothing like being ill and getting well to remind us to respect the body. The body has a consciousness of its own, and its own wisdom toward self-preservation.

In a recent bout with a stomach bug, my body stopped all activity in the interest of self-defense. I went along with no choice as my body purged all, totally releasing, in every way. There was a toxic invader and it was time to clear the decks to expel the enemy.

Without much else to do, I watched the process with a spiritual perspective. I noticed the wisdom of the body to let go without hesitation. I don't always do that. When something is toxic in my life, I've been known to hold on, trying to make it better. Maybe you do too. Have you held on to a job, relationship or situation long after it was done? Trying to make it better, or perhaps making it wrong or "the problem" as you mustered up the courage to create change?

Anyway, in this digestive adventure, nothing but the body and its well-being mattered for three days straight. Then, early on the fourth morning, I caught myself noticing the deep blue of the sky at dawn and the chattering birds out back. I went outside just at sunrise in the cool air, getting back to my usual summer morning routine. **The body's consciousness, having done its job, receded into the background once more.** There was space for me again. Thank you, body.

What About Bigger Stuff?

I'm talking about a simple stomach bug here, but what about significant illnesses? What an opportunity to bring stark clarity to the value of a body. Many people who survive a health crisis shift perspective. They worry less, love more and enjoy being alive. You can create that change without getting struck by lightning or surviving cancer. You're doing it right now.

One more note here. When an energy becomes physical and is expressing in the body as an illness, it's best to address it from both energetic and physical perspectives. It's important to look at the vibrations reflected in the illness and equally important to treat it with the wonderful resources medical science provides.

Remember the concept of metaphysical religion? That dogma would say you should be able to heal yourself with energy only. And, those spontaneous healings do happen on occasion. Yet, there's no sin in taking advantage of health care options. I've worked with too many people who won't even take an aspirin because it means they aren't doing their spiritual work. God created both herbs and Advil. You get to choose what's right for you.

Life Is Good

You created that body of yours by agreement with your biological parents. It's your transportation device, your sensory device and a communication mechanism.

Sometimes folks get into a mind-set that incarnation is a punishment, and we'll feel better or freer when it's over. That's just spiritual amnesia talking.

Living is where the action is and where the learning is. Incarnation is our highest achievement as spirit. And, you need a body to do it.

Walking in two worlds, free of the fog, we can see that the physical vessel is our greatest creation. It's the answer to your highest prayer as Spirit Self.

Culture of Judgment

But here we are, in a culture where body judgment is pervasive, especially for women. Women are natural nurturers and protectors. We're also natural improvers.

We've discussed this earlier in Living Spiritual Awareness – Chapter 5: The Crisis for Women. We naturally want to make things better. This tendency is cruelly used against us in the culture to seek a perfection in the body that isn't realistic or even possible for most humans.

If you've aligned with a spiritual practice, you may consider yourself immune, but think about it. When you look in the mirror, what's the thought stream? Is it, "hello beautiful" or "hooray for having a body." I'm betting not. How many thoughts do you have that are against your body? Imagine how your body, with its own consciousness, must feel.

The Creator

Your relationship with, and communication toward your body matters more than you might realize. You are your body's creator. Think about it; in a very real way, **you are God to your body**. Your recognition, appreciate and validation is your body's greatest gift. Your judgment is its greatest punishment; failure in the eyes of the creator. The body will respond accordingly to whatever energy it receives from you.

Interestingly, the devaluing of the physical form is yet another symptom of spiritual amnesia. When we don't acknowledge spirit, nothing is sacred or revered. The beautiful temple of the soul, the body, is cheapened. Notice how many young women, keepers of the magical cycle of incarnation, judge theirs so harshly and give them so freely.

Hello Water

A quick way to come out of judgment and change the energy in the body is to simply say hello to the water in your body. I know it sounds a little weird, as many effective spiritual exercises do, but why not?

Water is the physical element most sensitive to vibration. Focused intention and energy directed through thought create vibration and can change water. If you haven't seen the work of Dr. Masaru Emoto, check it out. He's demonstrating the amazing power of the human consciousness and its interactions with water. Truly incredible, eye-opening work.

Our bodies are composed of mostly of water, up to 70% depending upon age. Water, including the water in our bodies, senses vibration and records its findings in its own molecular structure. Water retains memory and then releases it when it changes states, freezing into ice, dispersing into vapor and coagulating again.

Water also responds to energy. We can change the vibration and memory of the water in our bodies by directing energy through focused thought toward it.

If you judge your body, as cultural paradigm would have you do, you are setting the water in your body at whatever you are throwing at it on a vibrational level. Perhaps you think of your body as ugly, fat, not good enough or all of the above. The water inside you is recording all of that.

To create a different experience, let yourself be a little goofy and think some nice thoughts toward the water in your body. How about: "Thank you water" or "Thank you body." Or, if you're feeling bold: "I love you water" or "I love you body."

Take a break from reading, close your eyes, ground and try it now.

Did you notice a shift in how you feel?

Think of an energy you'd like to give the water in your body in order to shift its molecular structure. Maybe love, health, vitality or joy? Stop here and give your body a gold sun of whatever vibration you choose. Imagine the golden light filling the water molecules inside you. Notice how this feels.

Changing energy is so simple. Sometimes I think it would be easier if there were a hard and arduous process to follow. People seem to give those types of things more validity.

At the end of this chapter, I've included two more fun and easy meditations for the body.

Eternity and Finality

Most people fear death. That dread is a symptom of spiritual amnesia. We've forgotten that death is a doorway. A way for us to change form, like water does.

Resistance to death is also a healthy perspective from the body's point of view. Of course the body wants to persist as long as possible.

When we can accept that death is inevitable and natural, we can appreciate the body even more. We can see it as the unique creation that it is.

You as soul are eternal, but that body is a one-time-only event.

Walking in two worlds, we can savor the uniqueness of the current life while grounding our sense of ourselves in the timeless realm. It's the perfect harmony of Spirit Self and Human Self.

Thought Stream Meditation

Before walking through the steps below, find your space by meditating. Follow the process outlined in Chapter 6 of Part 1 to ground and get your energy flowing. Connect with your Spirit Self by meditating before continuing on.

First, Just Notice
• Become aware of your body.
• Say hello to systems and the miraculous way they work together.
• Notice what thought is most prevalent in your Universe – for example, "I don't have enough money."
• Notice what energy is behind the thought – fear or doubt?

• Notice how your body responds to the thought and energy – stress? Illness?

Clean Out
• Clean out the energy using containers to collect and release it.
• Clean out the thought in the same way. Imagine letting the thought come out of your head, putting it in a container, releasing and destroying it.

Create Something New and Fill In
• Think a new thought you'd like to experience. Practice the new thought by thinking it repeatedly.
• Notice the energy behind the new thought. Is it self-love? Joy? Peace? Something else?
• Give yourself gold suns of the new energy.

Last, Just Notice
• Notice how your body responds to the new thought and new energy.
• Notice that you can change your condition.
• Own that power and use it wisely.

Here's another meditation for the body. This one is an eyes-open exercise.

Mirror Meditation

Ground yourself before you start and stay grounded as you move through the process. The grounding will help you release energies that come up.

Look at Your Body and Notice

- Stand naked before a full-length mirror. Look at your body.
- Notice the thoughts that come up. Don't engage with them, just notice them.
- Notice the energy or energies behind the thoughts – Self-judgment? Invalidation? Self-doubt? Something else?

Release, Replace and Notice the Shift
- Release both the thoughts and the energies.
   o Put the thoughts in containers, release and destroy them.
   o Put the energies in containers, release and destroy them.
- Think a new, loving thought toward your body. Force it at first, even if it feels untrue. Keep thinking the new thought.
- Notice the energy represented by the new thought – Self-love? Trust? Truth?
- Bring in gold suns of the new energy – lots of them!
- Notice the shift.

Don't stay stuck in the cultural program to hate your body – be a force for change from the inside-out!

WALKING IN TWO WORLDS

CHAPTER 2: MONEY

For most people, money is the most volatile topic of all. Those who've had life-threatening health challenges might be the only exception.

We address money, and other potentially explosive topics, in our spiritual development programs at the Inner Connection Institute. When we do, we meditate deeply on the subject. We allow buttons to get pushed using gentle techniques, so we can find the buttons. Buttons usually point to energies that control our experience. Once we become aware of the energies, we change them if we'd like.

As you read this chapter about money, notice if you feel resistance, defensiveness or confusion. These feelings may be the product of outmoded beliefs. Just underneath these initial reactions, there could be energies bubbling up to conscious awareness for cleansing. If your first response to something is "no way," please take a breath, ground and just look at whatever idea has raised your ire.

Maybe after some consideration, you just disagree. Disagreement is one way to find our own truth. But maybe there's something there for you.

One of our students, Kelle, says when she resists something right away, that's a sure sign for her that there's something in it for her to look at and learn from. As you can imagine, she's a delight to have in the group.

In class, when someone gets fired up about a topic and there's a lot of emotional energy, we say that person is "lit up." In a light up, deep-rooted beliefs are challenged and old energy surfaces. The person creates an opportunity for large-scale change, although there is discomfort in the moment.

This can happen around money. I'm concerned about you as you sit there reading, by yourself. You might get "lit up" without other people around to help you process the flux and harness it to support your transformation.

I don't know that there's much I can do from here. I do know I don't want to hold back, skate the surface or sugar-coat the subject.

You've got the tools to manage any light up. And, I'm available to you if you need me. See the chapter at the end of this book titled "What Now?" for ways to get in touch.

Please keep in mind that money is a hot topic for almost everyone. Your response to information about money, or any subject, is a reflection of the energies and beliefs you carry. If you get lit up as you read, use your Meditation for Living tools to find clarity, calm and your own truth.

If you don't like the current experience of money in your life, give yourself space to notice what's within you that creates the experience. And, give yourself the freedom to manifest differently by changing your energy. You know how; by using your Meditation for Living skills.

As you do, be gentle. Come to the topic with an open mind, some curiosity and more than a little spiritual amusement. In fact, let's stop here, ground and bring in a gold sun of amusement right now.

Feels good, doesn't it?

Let's just play with some concepts around money and allow any needed change to unfold in a graceful way.

What is Money?

Money is a way we manage the physical objects and resources of this physical reality. Prosperity creates choices. Generally, the more money a person has, the more options they have. If I'm hungry, I'm going to eat. I might eat at a shelter kitchen, a food bank, a fast food joint, a nice neighborhood restaurant or a swanky high-priced place, depending on money.

If I'm going on vacation, my level of prosperity may determine my destination and mode of travel. If I've got a lot of money, I have more options on how to spend my time than if I'm lacking abundance.

Having money is great! Plenty of it helps us feel secure, free and more joyous on the adventure of life.

Most people worry about money, or feel they don't have enough. We all deserve a graceful flow of abundance, so let's explore some energies that might restrict prosperity.

Keeping Clear Perspective

Money is a third chakra consideration. We talked about chakras way back in Experiencing Spiritual Awareness - Chapter 4: Chakras. To review, the third carries information about our personal power, will and drive. I like to call it the action chakra, or the do-er.

Many people believe they would die without money. That's not true. You would die without air, water, food or protection from the elements, but not money. Associating money with death makes it feel like a first chakra consideration and causes undue survival fears.

When survival is on the line, the first chakra focuses intently in a narrow fashion. Think of running from a tiger or jumping out of the way of an oncoming bus. Nothing else is real in that moment.

Being overly fearful about money can restrict its flow. If we create first chakra fear around money, we can easily get way too overstressed. In that condition, creativity actually narrows. In our desperation we won't feel powerful, and may not see all the possibilities before us.

Money is important, but it's not a life-or-death matter. In fact, it is one of the most replaceable commodities. If you lose what you have, you can recreate it, much more easily that you can your health.

When we have money in proper perspective, as a third chakra concept, we can feel safer about exploring it.

Everyone comes to the concept of money with a set of beliefs and, very likely, fears they've picked up along the human journey.

Money as a Space

So far in our exploration of energy, we've been talking about our space in a defined way: the body, chakras and aura. The information we carry in these areas is reflected back to us in our experience of life.

We can also look at particular information sets manifesting through specific facets of life. For example, our health, wealth, work and relationships. Each is a space of its own in a way. We may have certain beliefs, or pictures, expressing in our "money space" and others being played out in our health space.

We're busy beings on this human journey. Most of us have a lot of different spaces through which we express information.

You may have a parenting space, for instance. Most all of us have a driving space, and that can be an interesting one. Think about your food space as well. Most folks express much more energy there than the body's need for nutrition. Food can easily become a vehicle for the repression of pain. Pain is expressed in the relationship with food, or the "food space."

Looking at these various aspects of our non-physical space and exploring them is a great way to support yourself in living awake, to notice what you're creating and master proactive manifestation.

There are a few common energies that tend to be present in the money space and limit abundance. They may seem like just "what's true." In fact they are underlying vibrations that influence experience.

Families and Other Influences

One energy influencing the money space is family energy. Many people carry beliefs passed down from parents or other family members about how much money they can have, can't have and how to manifest abundance.

There can even be karmic considerations about money. Imagine being super rich, and wondering if the people around you really loved you or were just there for the money. You might intend, in the next lifetime, to not be super rich to free yourself to clear uncertainty around your lovability.

In present time, how we feel about ourselves and our life is reflected in our experience of money. If we feel fear, shame or guilt, we will withhold prosperity from ourselves without even realizing it.

When we are spiritually awake and feel good about who we are, we are much more open to all forms of flow, including prosperity. And, when we know ourselves to be both human and spirit, we are less likely to give our self-esteem away to money.

Yes, money is great, and we all deserve plenty. But it doesn't bring happiness. Happiness comes from a sense of self, not what we possess. For some, especially us self-employed folks, money comes and goes.

When we let money define how we see ourselves, we've given it too much power.

With spiritual perspective, we can take our power back from money and become its master instead of its slave.

Sometimes there is a shame about money itself. As if having money makes you greedy or not a good person. The wealthy are both vilified and envied these days.

People on a spiritual path often encounter an energy that would say, "Money isn't spiritual," as if it's not ok to have or desire money if you are a person interested in the expansion of consciousness. That is a silly energy.

Perhaps it's born of the old Catholic Church paradigm where the Church seems to have a lot but its servants have little. In part, that's a corruption of the teachings of Jesus. He sent the apostles out on mission without any possessions. That lesson is about trust and about letting go of validation from things. It wasn't a teaching that poverty is good or "higher."

Many women carry what I call the "on-the-street picture." The on-the-street picture is a fear of being destitute, homeless and alone. This picture isn't about money; it's about abandonment. The fear is about being rejected and deserted, rather than broke.

If these vibrations, or other limiting energies, are sitting in your money space, they will affect your financial manifestations. Imagine what would happen if you were to replace them with supportive energies like havingness and ease.

Let's do that right now! Let's go into a meditation here, and create some change. We'll be doing something new in the second exercise below, so remember to be in that space of play and curiosity, rather than effort and trying. You'll get a better result and you'll be more likely to stick with it.

Two Money Space Meditations

Before walking through the steps below, find your space by meditating. Follow the process outlined in Chapter 6 of Part 1 to ground and get your energy flowing. Connect with your Spirit Self by meditating before continuing on.

A Simple Clean Out On Money

First, Just Notice
• While sitting in meditation, think about money. Or, create a rose before you to represent the concept of money.
• Notice what happens in your experience.

Find Neutrality
• If you get lit up, consider running neutral Earth and cosmic energy.
• Neutral Earth and cosmic energy is presented in Part 2; Living Spiritual Awareness – Chapter 4; Neutrality and Resistance.

Release and Replace
• If you become aware of worry, fear, guilt, shame or other unsupportive energies, clean them out of your space.

• Create a rose, bubble or balloon and imagine releasing the energy into the container.
• Let the container fill, release it and destroy it. Repeat as many times as you'd like.
• Replace the energy you just cleared out with gold suns of whatever you'd rather have.
• Suggested vibrations would be havingness, prosperity, trust, freedom, peace and contentment.
• When you are done, toss the rose representing money away and destroy it.
• Notice how your space has shifted.

The second meditation below takes us deeper into looking at the information manifesting in your experience of money.

A Deeper Cleanse: Clearing the Money Space

Look at a Bubble
• Imagine a bubble before you.
• Imagine that the bubble represents your money space and that it contains all the beliefs, energies and pictures that go into your experience of money.
• This is new, so just play with it. It's ok if you feel like you are thinking or if you feel confused — that's normal with a new technique.
• Simply sit with the bubble.

Find Neutrality
• If you get lit up, consider running neutral Earth and cosmic energy.
• Neutral Earth and cosmic energy is presented in Part 2; Living Spiritual Awareness – Chapter 4; Neutrality and Resistance.

Release and Replace
- If you notice emotions like worry or fear, go ahead and clear them.
- Create a container (a rose, balloon or bubble), fill it with the energy you'd like to release and let it go by tossing the container away and destroying it.
- Using a gold sun, fill yourself in with energies you'd rather have instead.

Work With the Bubble
- Ground the bubble. Imagine a grounding cord on the bottom of the bubble and extend that cord to the center of the Earth.
- Grounding the bubble will make it easier to be aware of what's in it.
- Intend that fear in the bubble flows down the grounding cord and to the center of the Earth for recycling.
- Alternatively, you could imagine a container outside the bubble (a rose, second bubble or balloon).
- Imagine moving fear from the bubble into the container, sort of like "click-and-drag" on your computer.
- Repeat the previous step for any of the following energies you feel might be influencing you:
  o Family limitations
  o Guilt
  o Worry
  o Shame
  o Energy that says "money isn't spiritual"
  o Punishment energy (if you have money, you aren't a good person)
  o The on-the-street picture
  o Notice any other unsupportive energies you may have in your money space and clear them.

▪ This may include other people's energies. Go ahead and clear them with containers so you make more space for your own truth in your experience of money.

Own and Set the Money Space

• After you've cleared out this money bubble, imagine owning it with your own energy – that's just a simple intention.

• Next, fill in the sphere with gold suns of energies you'd like to experience in your money space. See a gold sun above the money sphere, set it at a vibration with a word and then set it into the bubble or pop it and watch the energy stream into the sphere. Here are some examples of energies you might want in your money space:

   o Havingness
   o Prosperity
   o Ease
   o Fun
   o Abundance

• Give yourself a gold sun of each of the energies you put in your money bubble.

• Imagine a rose next to the sphere and put the sphere in the rose.

• There are three options for taking the rose to its next step.

• You could plant the rose in your aura as a reminder.

• You could make the rose a mock-up (See Part 2; Chapter 2, Intention and Manifestation for the mock-up technique).

• You could simply toss the rose away and destroy it, trusting you've created the energetic shift.

Go Even Deeper?

• If you'd like, you could take this meditation to an even deeper level by mocking-up you in the condition of prosperity. You don't have to know how this will unfold. Simply see yourself in financial abundance and create a mock-up from that image. If it would feel rushed to do that now, you could come back and revisit when you have time to be relaxed and at ease.

Good job! Consciously choosing the energies influencing your money space will make a positive difference in your experience. You might want to repeat this meditation as often as feels right to you. The repetition will help you hold the new vibrations and release even more deep-seated limitations.

Do Try This on Other Spaces

Also, notice that you can apply this technique of looking at a bubble for a space to any facet of your life. You might want to clean out and reset your health space, for example. In the next chapter, we'll transform your work space.

WALKING IN TWO WORLDS

CHAPTER 3: WORK

Work and money are related, but they are two distinct spaces. Money can come from other sources besides work, and some people work without financial compensation.

Like money, work can be a hot topic when it's a challenge, so let's remember that space of curiosity and play as we dive in. If you get lit up as you read, use your meditation tools to unearth the energy surfacing, clear it and come to your own truth.

What is Work?

Ideally, work is a space through which we express ourselves.

We are each a unique manifestation of the all-one consciousness, an irreplaceable expression of God. We each bring our own contributions and talents to Earth, and ideally we express those gifts and abilities through our work in the world.

Mark Twain said, "Make your vacation your vocation." Do what you love.

So what happened? Why are so many people spending the day in places they'd rather not be in, doing what they'd rather not do and feeling stuck? There are a variety of reasons.

Young Minds

In the flow of our educational system, many people make decisions about their career before they really know themselves. We make monumental choices about our futures, and perhaps spend lots of money on education, all before our brains are fully developed. It's no wonder so many folks go to school, join the work world and then become frustrated.

Some create a whole new path more in alignment with who they are. Others may stick with the plan and that space of discontent, waiting it out for retirement to be free.

Of course, there are some who find a soul-fulfilling path right away and stay in it happily for a lifetime. A friend of mine from high school developed scoliosis as a teen. She became a chiropractor and has been joyous in that line of work ever since.

I, on the other hand, became an administrative assistant and then a computer programmer. Following my father's advice, this trajectory was a good idea at the time. I needed to support myself.

As I've mentioned before, I fell into the role of "office therapist" at each workplace. This pattern continued until my true work became clear.

Cultural Programming

Our families and society instill us with energies that influence work. Family dynamics often determine the type of work we are encouraged toward or away from. What's expected, acceptable or unacceptable in the family or group can have an enormous impact on our perceptions of our options, and on our choices.

Cultural energies matter too. For example, in many circles there's an undercurrent that work is painful, and then you get a break on the weekend. This energy would say you have to do what you don't want in order to have what you want. That "no pain, no gain" paradigm.

How about "no pain, no pain?" Seems almost sinful, doesn't it? Consider the idea of receiving for being in joy rather than suffering.

Sure, most all work has challenges. There are facets about managing the organization I run that aren't all that fun for me. I'd certainly rather be working with a client than catching up on the accounting. But overall, I know I'm working in alignment with my soul journey, my values and my path. It's a joyous adventure!

How about you? **Do you like your work or do you watch the clock?** Is what you do an expression of your values and joys as a spiritual being? Or, is it something you just fell in to?

As you wake from spiritual amnesia, you'll begin to recognize your abilities and your contributions. You'll be sparked by the desires of the soul as you open to who you truly are. As you do, you can use your Meditation for

Living tools to shift your experience of work. I've included a meditation at the end of this chapter to support you in the transition.

Jobs: Enjoying the One You Have Now

As many of us have experienced, working at a place that isn't right for you leads to mental, emotional and physical exhaustion. Stress levels increase dramatically when we don't like our job, and that creates all kinds of trouble.

Still, as you move toward your passion, it probably won't go well if you quit your job today and begin your singing career (or whatever is your passion), even though that might feel like a great idea in the moment. Likely, it's better to create a transition, moving toward what you'd like without throwing out what you have.

So, in the meantime, how do you enjoy a job that's not your passion? Author Mary Engelbreit says, "Bloom where you're planted." Mary also shares, "Walk toward the sunshine and the shadows will fall behind you."

Even if you don't like your job, it is possible to be more satisfied where you are as you simultaneously open to change. In fact, being more happy in your current position will accelerate your journey toward work you love. You'll be more content, vibrant, energetically attractive and open to broader options and possibilities.

You may be thinking, "How can I possibly do that?" Well, you can reframe your relationship to your current situation. What we tell ourselves about what is happening goes a long way in defining our experience.

Here are a couple of suggestions for bringing more enjoyment into what might be unsatisfying circumstances.

Stay Awake

Work is an important aspect of life, but it doesn't define your identity. When you are awake, your sense of self is grounded in knowing yourself as a spiritual being. In an unfulfilling workplace, that's easy to forget.

So, create a way to remind yourself. Of course, I'm a fan of daily meditation, even if it's for just a short piece of time. Perhaps you could also listen to inspiring recordings in your car or have regular talks with a like-minded friend.

This current moment is only a small part of your journey. What you do is not who you are. It is only an expression of you, or not!

Interestingly, it's also easy to forget our spiritual foundation if we are extremely successful at work. If you enjoy what you do, that's wonderful! Still, please don't give your sense of self over to your work. If the economy takes a dive (again), or if your industry collapses, will you be ok with yourself?

Some people pour their energy into careers, work extremely hard and amass success, only to find hollowness inside. Career success, like financial prosperity, is gratifying. The two can be a sweet treat in life. But, they are no substitute for spiritual fulfillment.

Make It Your Own

Another way to "bloom where you're planted" is to make your work your own. Even if your current job isn't your true calling, you can do it with self-expression and be uniquely you.

Whether it's the way you interact kindly with others or the integrity you bring to the most mundane of tasks, you can express your individuality. As you do, you'll feel more joy in any workplace. And, that shift will support you in creating and attracting a career that's more in line with who you are.

Practice Having Instead of Having To

Do you feel like you "have to" work? Most folks do. Many people see work as a burden or punishment. Havingness transforms this depressing mind-set. Imagine the attitude "I have work to do," rather than "I have to work."

That may seem like a stretch. Consider this idea: "I have a house to clean" instead of "I have to clean the house."

Having a house to clean is validating. Having a house to clean is a statement of the joy of having the house itself. I'd rather have a house to clean than not have a house to clean.

In the same vein, sit with the idea that "I have work to do" instead of "I have to work." The transition helps us move toward gratitude and validation rather than resistance. This may not leave you jumping up and down about going to work, but it will make the day more fun and meaningful.

See It as a Choice

Really, you don't "have to" do anything. You could quit your job right now and then deal with the financial consequences of that decision. Everything we do is a choice once we're adults in the world.

It helps to notice that going to work is a choice you make each day. It might not be one you enjoy, but again, moving into more empowering vibrations instead of feeling stuck will help you create the change you desire.

Deal With the Others

The people we work with can be one of the most fun, or one of the most troublesome aspects of a job. People always come together by spiritual agreement. We talked about agreements in Part 2; Living Spiritual Awareness - Chapter 8.

I believe we rarely meet anyone for the first time. Most connections carry over from past lives, either with loving affinity or unbalanced karma. Sometimes it can be tricky to tell the difference between the two.

If someone at work is pushing your buttons, perhaps they are a friend in spirit who has come to show you where the buttons are and get you moving toward a life more in alignment with who you are. Or, maybe there is unresolved conflict from a previous life playing out in present time.

If you have a challenging co-worker, use your Meditation for Living skills to look at the agreement between the two of you (see the meditation outlined in Part 2; Living Spiritual Awareness - Chapter 8). Often, simply bringing awareness to the energies at play in a situation sparks the process of healing.

Also, family-of-origin issues frequently arise in the workplace. Old pain and patterns get played out in the group dynamics. If someone at work is behaving in a dysfunctional way, that pain probably started way in the past.

When we are spiritually awake, we can be accountable for our experience. And, we can see others in a new light. We can choose our response to someone in pain, especially when they are expressing it in an inappropriate way. Using our energy management tools (for example, grounding and the aura bubble), we can step out of the game and begin to make space for transformation.

Living consciously, we can keep our energies and our realities focused and clear, and create next steps for ourselves. When we're in the fog, it can easily look like it's all someone else's fault and we are stuck. We get bogged down in karmic games and limited realities. I know which reality I like better. How about you?

Dealing with Oppression

People often lament that they can't "be themselves" at their job, and it's usually true. Generally, not ALL of you is required (nor requested) in any work space. If you are meant to be a great singer, but have become an accountant, your belting out a tune probably isn't welcome in the sea of cubicles at the office. It's just not part of the agreement.

Agreement is different than oppression. If everyone was free to express the totality of self at work all the time, things could get pretty chaotic pretty fast. In the accounting office, you'd be singing, I'd be guiding meditations and someone else might be painting a mural on their cubical wall.

If you are feeling oppressed at work, it may help to take a look and see if there is true oppression or just a narrow agreement of what's acceptable.

If the limitations are by agreement, make sure you have other outlets in your life for all of you to be seen and heard. Maybe it's time to get out to the clubs at night and sing, beginning to create a brand new career that's really you. Moving toward your passion in your life, letting "the shadows fall behind you," gets you moving in the direction of your dreams.

If there is true oppression in your work environment and people aren't being treated with dignity, no matter what the task, it's very likely time to make a move. When the dynamics are such that there's no room for you to energetically breathe and misery is the prevailing vibration, get out of there and create a next step. Even if the next step isn't into the work you were meant to do, it is a step in the right direction and a step in taking care of yourself.

Be Gentle

If work is a challenging area for you, please be gentle on yourself with this topic. As with money, the answers may not be clear right away. Live with questions and don't insist on immediate answers. Perhaps sit with, "What do I love to do?" Or, "What is my work in the world?" Or simply, "What is my next step?" Live with some questions and see what begins to emerge in your awareness.

Your Work Space

In the last chapter I introduced the idea of spaces as facets of life; like money, parenting and food, to name a few. You have a set of beliefs, energies, and pictures that create your experience of work. That would be your work space.

By clearing your work space, you can become clearer on what your true path really is and what work would be fulfilling for you.

There are some common energies you might find in your work space, and there will probably be individual things you've picked up along the way on your journey of life. Let's take a look with meditation.

Work Space Meditation

This meditation is similar to the one in the previous chapter on money. This style of clean out can be adapted to any space you'd like to clear and shift.

Before walking through the steps below, find your space by meditating. Follow the process outlined in Chapter 6 of Part 1 to ground and get your energy flowing. Connect with your Spirit Self by meditating before continuing on.

First, Just Look
• Imagine a bubble before you.
• Imagine that the bubble represents your work space and that it contains all the beliefs, energies and pictures that go into your experience of work.
• Simply sit with the bubble.

Find Neutrality

• If you get lit up, consider running neutral Earth and cosmic energy.

• Neutral Earth and cosmic energy is presented in Part 2; Living Spiritual Awareness – Chapter 4; Neutrality and Resistance.

Release and Replace

• If you notice emotions like worry or fear, go ahead and clear them.

• Create a container (a rose, balloon or bubble), fill it with the energy you'd like to release and let it go by tossing the container away and destroying it.

• Using gold suns, fill yourself in with energies you'd rather have instead.

Work With the Bubble

• Ground the bubble. Imagine a grounding cord on the bottom of the bubble and extend that cord to the center of the Earth.

• Grounding the bubble will make it easier to be aware of what's in it.

• Intend that fear in the bubble flows down the grounding cord and to the center of the Earth for recycling.

• Alternatively, you could imagine a container outside the bubble (a rose, second bubble or balloon).

• Imagine moving fear from the bubble into the container, sort of like "click-and-drag" on your computer.

• Repeat the previous step for any of the following energies you feel might be influencing you:
    o Burden
    o Resistance
    o Worry
    o Oppression

o Check for regret (would have/should have/could have) energy in the work bubble. This energy would represent where you've judged yourself for decisions you've made along the way in your work life. Notice that you always made the best decision you could with the information you had at the time. Forgive yourself and let it go, so you can be more present now.

o Notice any other unsupportive energies you may have in your work space and clear them.

▪ This may include other people's energies. Go ahead and clear them with containers so you make more space for your own truth in your experience of work.

Own and Set the Work Space

• After you've cleared out this work bubble, imagine owning it with your own energy – that's just a simple intention.

• Next, fill in the sphere with gold suns of energies you'd like to experience in your work space. See a gold sun above the work sphere, set it at a vibration with a word and then set it into the bubble or pop it and watch the energy stream into the sphere. Here are some examples of energies you might want in your work space:

o Havingness
o Amusement
o Creativity
o Enthusiasm
o Abundance
o Prosperity
o Validation

• Give yourself a gold sun of each of the energies you put in your work bubble.

• Imagine a rose next to the bubble and put the sphere in the rose.

• There are three options for taking the rose to its next step.

• You could plant the rose in your aura as a reminder.

• You could make the rose a mock-up (See Part 2; Chapter 2, Intention and Manifestation for the mock-up technique).

• You could simply toss the rose away and destroy it, trusting you've created the energetic shift.

Go Even Deeper?

• If you'd like, you could take this meditation to an even deeper level by mocking up you doing work you love. You don't even have to know what that work is or how it might unfold. Simply see you loving your work. If you have some more detailed information to put in the mock up, that's great. At the same time, remember to keep it loose to allow the broadest range of possible manifestations. If it would feel rushed to do that now, you could come back and revisit when you have time to be relaxed and at ease.

WALKING IN TWO WORLDS

CHAPTER 4: RELATIONSHIPS

We round out our "Big Four" topics with relationships. I don't call them the Big Four for nothing! Health, money, work and relationships are major areas of life experience and all are rich with opportunities for self-awareness and spiritual growth.

Throughout this book, we've explored the energies we carry and beliefs we hold. In the last few chapters, we've looked at how those energies and beliefs play out in the Big Four areas of life.

It takes spiritual courage to look at, own and change one's reality. Shifting energy and beliefs involves giving up your story about how the past has defined you. You may find yourself letting go of resentments and judgments you've been carrying. If so, good for you!

Without the burden of outmoded beliefs, you're free to create a brand new reality in present time. You're moving into spiritual freedom.

On to Relationships

Like the other Big Four concepts, we can get lit up when looking at relationships. Sometimes it's hard to believe they all happen by agreement.

When two people create a relationship, they each contribute to the relationship between them according to their own histories and realities. Other foreign energies can influence the connection too.

In every relationship, we are giving and receiving, learning and teaching. Using the Meditation for Living techniques, we can clean out the relationship space and shift the spiritual contract. When we do, we give the other party or parties involved the freedom to respond to that shift.

These concepts and more involving our interactions with others were presented in Part 2; Chapter 8 – Living Spiritual Awareness; Families and Agreements. You can use the techniques in that section to look at any relationship.

I'm going to take this chapter in a direction you might not expect. When we suffer from spiritual amnesia, it seems that our connections with our spouses, family, friends and coworkers are the primary ones in life.

When we wake up spiritually, we see that the most important relationships are the one we have with ourselves and the one we have with the consciousness that creates this Universe (God, Spirit, or whatever you name that energy).

The most significant and transformative relationships you can cultivate are your relationship with yourself and your connection with the consciousness that creates this Universe. These relationships are reflected in all your other associations.

You and Yourself

Remember the chapter on chakras? We looked at these energy centers in Experiencing Spiritual Awareness: Chapter 4; Chakras. The fourth chakra carries information on how you see yourself.

Like all of reality, how you see yourself is based on a set of decisions. In this case, a set of conclusions about yourself. To change your relationship with you, change the decisions you've made about you.

For example, you may say in your own head that you are not good enough. You may believe that and it may feel very real.

However, that belief is founded in a decision you made about you. You can make a new decision and seed a new experience of yourself. Perhaps you have many reasons to back up your decision. Let them all go.

If you hold something against yourself from your history, please ease up on you. Very likely, you acted from the highest information you had at the time.

There was a time in my life when I was a heavy drug user and slept around. Those were the best coping skills I had during those years to handle deep pain and anxiety. Later, when I learned more, I stopped those behaviors. But

I'm not going to punish myself for them. It all seemed like a great idea at the time.

Mirror, Mirror

When you look in the mirror, what do you see? A beautiful expression of God? A unique and magnificent soul on a journey? Probably not. More likely, you see what you perceive to be flaws.

If you see yourself as broken, not good enough, unattractive, or unworthy, those vibrations will be reflected in your experiences. If you see yourself as whole, more than enough, beautiful, and deserving, you'll get those energies fed back to you by the Universe.

Are you your own best friend? Notice how you treat yourself in your inner thoughts and outward words. If you aren't good to you, you'll see that reflected in your relationships with others and in your relationship with your own health and wealth.

We will all be happy when we choose to be, not when something about us changes or external circumstances shift. Choose to build a relationship with yourself that supports your own happiness.

How? Well, **first you've got to stop being mean to you!** That's an important start. It might be a habit at this point, so be mindful of breaking it.

Start to say some nicer things to yourself. This may take practice and feel weird at first. Try this sometime soon (maybe right now): Stand in front of the mirror and notice your inner landscape of thought. Notice the thoughts that aren't nice to you. Ground yourself, find the center of your head and put those thoughts in a container, like a balloon. Blow them up. Don't answer them, justify them or argue with them. That just gives them more energy. Instead, simply let them go.

Next, practice a few new, kinder thoughts. It might be uncomfortable at first. For instance, you may choose the thought: "I am worthy, lovable and spectacular." That's a nice one! That decision would support happiness.

Think this new thought, or another one you choose, as you look at yourself. Say it out loud. I know that will be uncomfortable at first, but keep going. Continue and notice how your inner feelings begin to change. How great is that? As you practice a simple, new decision, you get a new experience.

Consider taking this practice into your daily life. Release unkind decisions by releasing the thought forms. Practice new thoughts, out loud too. If shame or fear comes up as you practice the new thoughts, use your Meditation for Living tools to clear them. The process will break energetic patterns and reset the information in the fourth chakra. You'll open to new vibrations and a broader range of possibilities.

You may also want to use your meditation skills to clean out a bubble representing your relationship with yourself. You could adapt the work space meditation from the previous chapter and apply the techniques to look at your relationship with yourself. You could clean out energies that don't support you and bring in vibrations that strengthen a more joyful life.

It truly is a matter of choosing and persisting in the new choice.

The Consciousness That Creates This Universe

Cultivating an awareness of the consciousness that creates this Universe is one of the most life-enhancing experiences you can give to yourself. You don't have to connect with the consciousness. You are already a part of it. You need only become aware of the consciousness of which you are a part.

It's a challenge to even approach this subject because it is steeped in dogma and superstition. Many religious paradigms would say that you can't connect directly with God, that you're not worthy. And, that you have to go through a middle-man, like a priest.

To counter this control, many folks have thrown out the concept of God altogether, to their own detriment.

A connection to God is a connection to yourself. You are an expression of the all-one consciousness, an irreplaceable piece of the puzzle. It's not the same Universe without you.

Knowing and experiencing yourself as a part of the whole brings a sense of fulfillment that can't be duplicated. The loss of this knowledge is at the core of spiritual amnesia.

People who've forgotten what they are, tend to try to replace the God connection with things from outside; money, fame, success, drugs, alcohol or food to name a few. Another tactic is to over-emphasize science and the intellectual realm.

A person once said to me, while discussing life after death, "If I can't see it, it's not real." In reply, I inquired about bacteria. At one point we couldn't see them, were they not real? Science helps us discover the world and engage with it. It's an important discipline, but can't replace the spiritual experience.

So many people walk their journey in emptiness and the pain of a void within. The void is filled with the awareness of oneself as spirit and as a unique part of the all-one consciousness.

That we are spirit never goes away, just the awareness is veiled. So, again, you don't need to connect with God, or become one with the consciousness that creates this Universe. You only need recognize that you already are.

Here's a meditation to get you started. It's a visceral thing, not a thinking process. Rather than talk about the experience, let's have it.

Hello God Meditation

We'll be working from the seventh (or crown) chakra toward the end of this mediation, rather than the center of head space. That's a new step, so please approach it with some playfulness and curiosity. If you don't like moving your attention to the crown, you can do the entire exercise from the center of your head.

Before walking through the steps below, find your space by meditating. Follow the process outlined in Chapter 6 of

Part 1 to ground and get your energy flowing. Connect with your Spirit Self by meditating before continuing on.

First, Just Look
- Imagine a bubble before you.
- Imagine that the bubble represents your relationship with the consciousness that creates this Universe, God, spirit or whatever you call that energy.
- Simply sit with the bubble.

Find Neutrality
- If you get lit up, come to neutrality by changing your Earth and cosmic energies to neutral colors (this technique is presented in LSA 4 Resistance and Neutrality).

Release and Replace
- If you notice emotions like grief or fear, go ahead and clear them.
- Create a container (a rose, balloon or bubble), fill it with the energy you'd like to release and let it go by tossing the container away and destroying it.
- Using a gold sun, fill yourself in with energies you'd rather have instead.

Work With the Bubble
- Ground the bubble. Imagine a grounding cord on the bottom of the bubble and extend that cord to the center of the Earth.
- Grounding the bubble will make it easier to be aware of what's in it.
- Intend that unconsciousness (energy that says either "this isn't real" or "don't look at this") in the bubble flows down the grounding cord and to the center of the Earth for recycling.

- Alternatively, you could imagine a container outside the bubble (a rose, second bubble or balloon).
- Imagine moving unconsciousness from the bubble into the container, sort of like "click-and-drag" on your computer.
- Repeat the previous step for any of the following energies you feel might be limiting your experience of yourself as a part of the whole:
  o Family limitations
  o Religious control
  o Unworthiness
  o Shame
  o Fear of being foolish (sort of an intellectual atheism)
  o Notice any other unsupportive energies you can see in your relationship with God and clear them.
    ▪ This may include other people's energies. Go ahead and clear them with containers so you make more space for your own truth in your experience of the consciousness that creates this Universe.

Own and Set the Space
- After you've cleared out this bubble, imagine owning it with your own energy – that's a simple intention. Also, imagine being open to a new experience in this realm of life.
- Next, fill in the sphere with gold suns of energies you'd like to experience in your relationship with God. You may not know what you'd like at this point, and that's ok. Here are some suggestions:
  o Havingness
  o Clarity
  o Joy
  o Love
  o Abundance

- Give yourself a gold sun of each of the energies you put in the bubble.
- Imagine a rose next to the sphere and put the sphere in the rose.
- There are three options for taking the rose to its next step.
- You could plant the rose in your aura as a reminder.
- You could make the rose a mock-up (See Part 2: Living Spiritual Awareness - Chapter 2: Intention and Manifestation for the mock-up technique).
- You could simply toss the rose away and destroy it, trusting you've created the energetic shift.

A New Step: Move Up to the Crown
- Notice you are in the middle of your head, that center of head space.
- Imagine looking up at your crown, or seventh, chakra.
- Let your attention float up from the middle of your head to the top of your head.
- Notice the difference in your experience, moving into the sense of knowingness present in the crown.
- You may want to practice moving from the center of your head to the crown and back again, just to play.

Say Hello
- While in the crown chakra, simply say, "Hello God," or "Hello Universe," or "Hello Spirit." Repeat the hello until you sense a shift.
- Notice what happens.
- Keep it simple and just be open. Let go of any expectation of what you'll feel and allow what is happening.
- You may notice a vibration, like a wave, or a background resonance of energy. You'll notice it

however you do. Since you are a unique part of the whole, your noticing will be unique to you.

    o You may find you don't hold neutrality while you say hello to the Universe and receive the resonance. That's fine! Let the joy, or whatever comes up for you, flow freely.

• Imagine opening to the vibration or resonance. Just receive and bask in it for as long as you'd like.

• Notice how the vibration fills you, and touches you within like nothing else can.

• When you're ready to come out of this meditation space, intend to bring this awareness into your sense of yourself as you move through your day (or whole life!).

The wave, vibration or resonance you experienced is with you all the time. It never stops. You simply took a moment to "tune in."

I encourage you to give yourself this experience frequently. I just took a break from writing and did it myself. What an amazing sensation. Taking the time to notice your connection to the consciousness that creates this Universe grounds your sense of yourself as an incarnated soul in an experiential way. You are awake!

WALKING IN TWO WORLDS

CHAPTER 5: TRAGEDIES AND MIRACLES

We've come a long way. At this stage of the journey, you're spiritually awake. And, you are equipped with a skill set to create your life. You know yourself as both Human Self and Spirit Self.

Perhaps you've already begun to cultivate a more joyous and abundant experience. Certainly, you're prepared for any trials ahead. Being awake doesn't mean there are no challenges. That's part of "metaphysical religion." **There's an unreachable myth that we could create a perfect vibration where no hardships ever occur.** That illusion mirrors the punishment and reward systems that have become so toxic in traditional worship.

As the character Larry said in the movie *The Razor's Edge*, "It's easy to be a holy man on top of a mountain." That's true. Brave souls go into town.

Earth isn't a planet of rest, it's a place of adventure and learning. It's not that nothing ever happens, it's what we do with it. Most importantly, what matters are the decisions we make about ourselves and our reality in response to life events.

Perhaps you were living in the fog of spiritual amnesia and had fallen into a pattern of dating irresponsible partners. Once you wake up, it's not that you'll never meet another immature date. It's that you'll recognize the dynamic and not jump into a relationship. And, you'll notice and clear the beliefs about yourself that attract that type of person. Pretty soon you'll be attracted to a new type of partner, and the attraction will be mutual.

As you live with your spiritual eyes open, problems will still come and go, but your expanded sense of yourself will make the difficulty seem smaller relative to your vision of yourself.

If you see yourself from only the human perspective, if you're spiritually asleep, let's say your sense of yourself is the size of a soccer ball. If a problem in your life is the size of a baseball, that challenge takes up a significant portion of your experience.

However, if you wake up, your sense of yourself expands as you know yourself as a spiritual being. Perhaps first to the size of a beach ball, then hot air balloon. And, you continue to see yourself as vaster and vaster still. Now, the baseball takes up a tiny fraction of your reality. It's the same problem, but it's not so big after all.

That which used to eat away at you will become not such a big deal. Spiritual awareness brings a lovely perspective.

But What About The Big Stuff?

Sometimes enormous challenges arise. Extreme financial loss, endings of relationships or career, illness or death can stretch our commitment to spiritual awareness to the brink. How do you handle the big stuff?

You know yourself as both Human Self and Spirit Self. Challenges are best addressed from both sides. If you approach a tragedy from the human perspective only, it is overwhelming. If you look only from spiritual perspective, that negates the human experience, and you won't truly move through it.

I recently did a reading for a woman who has had a debilitating spinal injury. She lost her business, her house, filed bankruptcy, lost both her dog and her best friend to death and developed a vision challenge; all in the last two years. From the human perspective, it's been beyond challenging and there's pain on every level. She's got to feel that and not stuff it.

From the spiritual view, she's created a blank canvas from which she can build a brand new life. She's invited herself to let go of the past and dive deeply into spiritual lessons she only skated the surface of before. As a soul, she's excited about the adventure ahead. Often, things look totally different in spirit than on Earth.

Spiritual awareness creates a space, a comfort in which the Human Self can move through even the roughest parts of the journey.

One of my nephews, Curt, was a troubled young man who passed at just twenty years of age. Curt never quite fit energetically in his body or in this physical realm.

It's been a major life tragedy for my sister (his mother) and the rest of the family. What a thing for a mom and dad to lose their son.

I spoke with Curt shortly after his passing. He showed me where he had been headed in human life; homeless, paranoid, on the street and my sister and brother-in-law in constant pain. As a soul, he chose to let go early and try again. So, on Earth, this is a terrible event. In spirit, all is well in the Universe, as always.

Speaking of Death

People tend to see every birth as a miracle and every death as a tragedy. Yet they are both parts of the same cycle. Certainly some deaths are more painful for those of us here on Earth than others. The young, the fallen soldiers, the suddenly ill. In the human experience, it feels so wrong, and in the human experience, it is. When we know that our loved one is not gone, but has only changed form, it helps.

The body is a vehicle for the soul to navigate the physical plane. No one wants to drive the same car for eternity. We learn and grow through a variety of experiences.

The other night I had a spectacular dream where I saw my mother, who just recently died. It started out in a beautiful wooded setting and evolved into some amazing flying experiences. In the dream I actually said, "I love dreams like this," as I floated above the trees to say hello to the stars. I won't bore you with the details, but suffice it to say I'll never forget that one.

After gently landing back on the ground, I turned and saw her. We exchanged joyful greetings and hugged. She radiated a particular energy: Reassurance. It was palpably strong. The message was clear, "I'm fine and all is well."

I woke instantly with total clarity and memory of the experience, for which I am so grateful. The night proceeded with a series of astral experiences of meeting family members I had never met in the human experience. What a gift. All these people are dead, yet here they are, very much alive and well in spirit.

Certainly, seemingly untimely deaths like my nephew's are extraordinarily painful for those experiencing the loss. We can let ourselves have, express and move through the pain surrounded by the comfort of spiritual perspective. In this way, we can handle it and maybe even create pieces of beauty as we heal a shattered heart.

Through the loss of their son, my sister and her husband have opened up to spiritual truth. They've spoken with Curt through mediums and have had experiences that have erased all previous atheism and skepticism they carried. They don't sweat the small stuff now, because they know for sure that the future is not only unknown, but also unknowable.

The Unknowable Future

Most people love a good prediction. This or that is going to happen in this or that particular time frame. As a reader and healer in the world, foretelling irritates me.

I've counseled many people recovering from predictive readings. They've gone into failure after the big promotion, marriage or windfall didn't unfold. I could go on and on about the problem with prediction. Clearly, I have some judgment about it!

The future is unknowable. We are creating it moment-to-moment through our beliefs, energies and free will. As we grow and change, the future we are creating shifts.

We do have intentions for particular lifetimes; experiences we want to explore, certain relationships to grow or release, specific vibrations to cultivate or discharge. But how it all plays out is wide open.

More Big Stuff

In another recent session, I worked with a women just getting out of a terribly abusive marriage of two years. She saw herself as "destroyed." We worked together to reframe the experience.

I saw her as wiser, not destroyed. In fact, she sat before me alive and well and fully capable of creating anew. When she began to see herself in that way, she let go of defining herself solely by this one short period of time in her life. I looked at the past lives between her and her ex and it all came clear in a brand new light.

I can't say enough that what we tell ourselves about a challenge, how we frame it, is so important in how it integrates into our sense of ourselves and our future creations. This is a crucial concept for living awake.

This lovely woman was willing to let me clear away the old and help her decide a new truth without insisting on sticking with an unhappy reality. She did a great job of releasing the story she was telling herself. So, together we created a brand new day and a brand new set of possibilities.

When significant challenges come on the journey of life, be open to the big picture. Yes, this or that is happening in the human experience. It's painful and that can't be, and shouldn't be, denied. At the same time, something is unfolding in spirit. Don't be too quick to decide what it all means. Stay as open as possible. I've included a meditation at the end of this chapter to support you in tough times.

I'm talking about that illusive thing called faith, a knowingness that there is purpose without an insistence that it all make sense in the moment.

A trust in spiritual truth without intellectual understanding opens us up to possibilities beyond what we've already decided is true. We move beyond the boundary of what we've allowed to be possible.

Beyond The Boundary: Miracles

We tend to call reality that which we've agreed is possible, but that's not all that is possible. When something happens outside the agreed-upon boundary of reality, we call it a miracle.

A miracle is an occurrence that is seemingly impossible according to the current perception of reality. By being open, with a willingness to be loose in our definition of what's possible, we allow miracles. As we experience them, our perception of reality expands.

I've experienced several wonders outside the boundary. Earlier, I shared about the miracle of the dimes. I'm open to the idea that anything can happen.

Years ago, I watched a pair of favorite earrings fall directly down the bathroom sink after I dropped them. I had bought them for myself as a statement of strength just after my first marriage ended.

I was upset on the human level, and I also knew that, since it happened, it must be time to let them go. A few weeks later, I opened my jewelry box and there they were sparkling at me.

I received them back with deep gratitude. I never pursued "why." I didn't dismantle the sink or try to figure it out. I just said thank you. **If I need it to make intellectual sense, I'm going to limit my possibilities to that which makes intellectual sense.** That's the last thing I want to do.

Instead, I stay open and watchful. The spiritual and physical realms are in a constant state of interaction. Beautiful things are happening around us all the time as consciousness unfolds into physical manifestation.

Another Type of Miracle

Sometimes what doesn't happen is the miracle. This type of miracle unfolded one day as I was working out at a local recreation center. As I released a pin on one of the machines, a weight that I hadn't noticed was loose dropped from above. I felt it brush the top of my head, go sideways toward my back, and fall behind me. That was interesting. The weight defied gravity. Instead of over-questioning, I simply said thank you to whoever brushed it away.

Another time my friend Cheryl, who I spoke of at the beginning of this book, came in to our office with a stunned look on her face. When I asked what happened, she described her miraculous drive to work. On our major highway here in Denver, she passed between two trucks when one swerved wildly. She was absolutely certain she'd be hit, and then was somehow suddenly driving in front of the trucks. That was a good one!

When we can have the truth that reality is much larger than our thinking minds can perceive, life gets more fun. We open up to realms within ourselves and in overall experience to create in phenomenal ways. Miracles are outside the box. I say, jump out. There's a lot to see out here.

To be more open to miracles, keep your energy clear by using your Meditation for Living skills. Also, frequently say hello to the consciousness that creates this Universe. Notice when you are telling yourself a story about something, and at least acknowledge that it is a story, not solid reality. Even better, let the story go and be open to new information.

There's no particular process to being open, it's more a stance of consciousness and belief. Know that reality is larger than the agreed-upon paradigm, and allow miracles to come your way. When they do, notice and say thank you. Your gratitude is like saying, "More of this, please."

Meditation for Times of Tragedy

Before walking through the steps below, find your space by meditating. Follow the process outlined in Chapter 6 of

Part 1 to ground and get your energy flowing. Connect with your Spirit Self by meditating before continuing on.

First, Just Look and Be With Yourself

• As you run your energy, let any feelings come up. Rather than resist, let them flow up and through you. If you'd like, create and destroy roses as you release on an emotional level. Eventually, the body will reach a state of completion with this, at least for now.

• Reset yourself in the center of your head after any emotions have passed.

• Create a rose to represent the current situation. Just look at it for a moment.

Find Neutrality? Maybe.

• You may want to attempt to come to neutrality by changing your Earth and cosmic energies to neutral colors (this technique is presented in LSA 4 Resistance and Neutrality).

• This may or may not work, or even be appropriate, in a time of great challenge. Be gentle with yourself.

Notice, Release and Replace

• Notice if you've been creating a story in response to what's happening. Are you making decisions about yourself or about reality that don't support the life you'd like to create?

• If you are, imagine releasing those decisions into a container, moving them out of your space and destroying the container; neutralizing and dissipating the energy.

• Fill yourself in with gold suns of what you'd rather have, perhaps self-love, peace, havingness or clarity. You could even fill in with some amusement. Spiritual amusement brings perspective even in the darkest hour, even though it may seem inappropriate at the time.

Let It Go and Open Up

• Imagine giving the rose that represents the current situation to God. You could sit with this idea if you like, "Thank you God that this has unfolded to the highest good."

• Let the rose go to the consciousness that creates this Universe. If you find yourself taking the rose back, simply release it again.

• Sit with the idea of being open. There's more going on here than meets the eye, or mind. Allow yourself to know this without having to have it all figured out right now.

Say Hello if You'd Like

• You might want to say hello to God (as described in the previous chapter). It's always an expansive experience:

  ○ Imagine looking up at your crown, or seventh, chakra.

  ○ Let your attention float up from the middle of your head to the top of your head.

    ▪ Notice the difference in your experience, moving into the sense of knowingness present in the crown.

  ○ You may want to practice moving from the center of your head to the crown and back again, just to play.

• While in the crown chakra, simply say, "Hello God," or "Hello Universe," or "Hello Spirit." Repeat the hello until you sense a shift.

• Notice what happens.

• Keep it simple and just be open. Let go of any expectation of what you'll feel and allow what is happening.

• You may notice a vibration, like a wave, or a background resonance of energy. You'll notice it however you do. Since you are a unique part of the whole, your noticing will be unique to you.

Bask in the Resonance
• Imagine opening to the vibration or resonance. Just receive and bask in it for as long as you'd like.
• Notice how the vibration fills you, and touches you within like nothing else can.
• When you're ready to come out of this meditation space, intend to bring this awareness into your sense of yourself as you move through your challenge.

WALKING IN TWO WORLDS

CHAPTER 6: SPIRITUAL FREEDOM

When we wake from amnesia, live with awareness and walk in two worlds, we experience spiritual freedom.

Spiritual Freedom is the capacity to choose one's energy and reality.

From Helpless to Healer

As you can tell from what I've shared with you of my own journey, my life has not always been an easy one this time around. The cycles of abuse and molestation my mother experienced in her family continued, as cycles often do.

To survive as a child, I kept my skills of remote viewing and astral travel sharp. When I became a young woman, the pain festered deep within. In my darkest days, I relied on alcohol, drugs and sex to feel alive, stuff the hurt and manage anxiety.

Through a series of divine synchronicities I now recognize were orchestrated by my Spirit Self, I woke up.

With the support and wisdom of great teachers, I have come to know myself and become a catalyst of transformation for others. I've gone from helpless to healer, and so can you.

I know from personal experience and from supporting the journeys of others for over twenty years that any experience can be reframed, any wound healed, any darkness transformed by the light of spiritual truth.

Your path may not look like mine, but you can go from wherever you are to wherever you'd like. You can discover who you are on the human level and what you are on the spiritual plane.

You can live joyously as your Human Self and Spirit Self dance together along the path of life. You can have that inner peace that comes from living awake. You can express and contribute in a way that is fulfilling and meaningful for you.

It takes divine courage, spiritual skill and willingness. Check, check and check! You're already on your way.

The Three Keys

Remember way back at the beginning of our journey together? I described heaven as the condition of knowing oneself in totality, as a soul, as a being of light, a part of the all-one consciousness and at the same time, unique. The condition of heaven brings spiritual freedom.

I'm sure you've noticed that I'm not a fan of traditional religious paradigms. Yet, there are lovely nuggets of truth hidden among the control games. We can enjoy the gems without the toxicity.

One of my favorites from the Christian tradition is the keys to the kingdom of heaven. There are three: know thyself, come as a little child and be reborn again.

When we take a fresh look at these concepts, we see that they really are the keys to the condition of heaven on Earth.

First, know thyself. Know yourself to be an incarnated soul on the journey of life. When we know ourselves to be that; a spiritual being in human experience, everything looks, feels and is different. That peace and joy are right there.

Second, come as a little child. A little child hasn't made any decisions about reality yet. And, a healthy child has a spirit of adventure and an assumption that life is good unless they are taught otherwise. The natural energy is toward fun and contentment. So, approach the journey of life with a spirit of adventure, some spiritual amusement and the knowledge that all is well in the Universe.

Last, to be reborn again. To be reborn is to let go of the past. More importantly, let go of the decisions you've made about yourself and life based on the past. If you don't enjoy the reality those decisions are generating, change them. And, of course, you don't have to go through someone else to be energetically cleansed. It's your choice.

I wish you heaven on Earth. You deserve nothing less. You have the keys to your own inner kingdom of reality. Open the door.

WALKING IN TWO WORLDS

CHAPTER 7: WHAT NOW?

We're nearing the end of this leg of our journey. You now know you are a spiritual being on the human adventure, free to create reality as you choose.

My hope is that you'll continue to live awake and aware, creating your own heaven on Earth.

As you do, you manifest your own personal transformation. And, you contribute to an environment of permission for others to do the same. Thank you for helping change the world by shifting yourself.

Where do we go from here? If you'd like to continue your journey with me by your side, I'm here to support you.

Please visit my website, www.laurenskye.com. I have several options for continuing your exploration of yourself and of energy management skills listed there. There are classes by telephone or download, and in-person events. I also provide private energetic reading and healing sessions to help you jump-start your reality.

I'd be honored to work with you in a class space or personal session. I mean it. There's nothing more precious to me than supporting you. Your uniqueness is needed. You can contact me through the site or at lauren@laurenskye.com. Know that I welcome your communication and look forward to hearing from you.

My offerings and the website are an ever-evolving thing. Please do sign up for my mailings (you can always unsubscribe). Or, check the website from time to time.

Right now, one item on the site is a free e-book, *Believing is Seeing*. It's a fun collection of essays that will help you remember. I hope you'll download and enjoy.

There's also a spot on the site to register as a meditator. You can click there and fill out a short form to receive tips for using the Meditation for Living skills and special offers on my services. Use the code "sarose118" to complete the form.

Also, remember that you can e-mail me or sign up for my newsletter from the website to receive the full first lesson of the audio series, Meditation for Living: New Life Skills For Everyone, at no charge. The complete seven-lesson series walks you through all the skills presented here and also includes morning and evening meditations as well as a thorough practice walk-through.

More Thoughts on Staying Awake

For best results, use your tools. Make meditation a part of your life. I know it's hard to do anything daily, but keeping up your practice with as much frequency as works in your life will keep you clear. Think of meditation like an energy shower. It's part of your self-care. It feels good to get clean.

Also, you could give yourself little reminders. Put a little sketch of a gold sun on your refrigerator, car dash board or bathroom mirror. Or, put this book somewhere where you'll see it as a cue to ground. If you've downloaded this text, perhaps print one page of your favorite chapter or take a screen shot of it.

Find Like-Minded Others

Explore your community for support. Groups exploring spiritual truth without religious control are popping up all over. At the same time, do be careful out there! Not everyone involved in this work is walking the talk. If it doesn't feel right, or if there are control games, look elsewhere.

Use time and attention wisely. Your time and your attention are two of your most precious resources in this lifetime. Be mindful to spend them on activities and people who support you in living awake and being fully you.

Until We Meet Again

I appreciate your time and attention in reading this book. May you enjoy this life and enjoy being you.

WITH JOYOUS THANKS...

For the many teachers I've been blessed to learn from
For the many students I've been honored to teach
And for the many more of both to come

WITH DEEPEST GRATITUDE...

For Berny and Sarah
For Margaret
And for Bruce Wayne, the Dog of Joy

ABOUT THE AUTHOR

Lauren Skye is a professional meditation facilitator and spiritual development educator in practice since 1994. She also offers private intuitive reading and energy healing sessions combining a variety of modalities to effect healing and change. Lauren is the founder of the Inner Connection Institute, a Colorado non-profit organization since 1996.

Lauren's work is all about empowering you to create the life you desire; the life that is a reflection of your true self and spirit, with your optimal capacity for health, love, prosperity and joy.

To learn more, please visit **www.laurenskye.com**.

51428400R00141

Made in the USA
San Bernardino, CA
22 July 2017